Introduction to
the Synoptic Gospels

Introduction to
the Synoptic Gospels

under the supervision of
Richard P. Thompson

Theological Essentials

©Digital Theological Library 2025

Library of Congress Cataloging-in-Publication Data

Richard P. Thompson (creator).
Introduction to the Synoptic Gospels / Richard P. Thompson
109 + x pp. cm. 12.7 x 20.32
ISBN 979-8-89731-200-9 (Print)
ISBN 979-8-89731-117-0 (Ebook)
ISBN 979-8-89731-115-6 (Kindle)
ISBN 979-8-89731-116-3 (Abridged Audio Discussion)

   1. Synoptic Gospels—Criticism, interpretation, etc.
   2. Bible. N.T. Gospels—Criticism, interpretation, etc.

BS2555 .T46 2025

***This book is available in other languages at
www.DTLPress.com***

Cover Image: Stained glass window from Wesley Chapel,
London, "Parable of the Sower"
Photo credit: DTL Staff

Contents

Series Preface

Artificial Intelligence (AI) is changing everything, including theological scholarship and education. This series, *Theological Essentials*, is designed to bring the creative potential of AI to the field of theological education. In the traditional model, a scholar with both mastery of the scholarly discourse and a record of successful classroom teaching would spend several months—or even several years—writing, revising and rewriting an introductory text which would then be transferred to a publisher who also invested months or years in production processes. Even though the end product was typically quite predictable, this slow and expensive process caused the prices of textbooks to balloon. As a result, students in developed nations paid more than they should have for the books and students in developing nations typically had no access to these (cost-prohibitive) textbooks until they appeared as discards and donations decades later. In previous generations, the need for quality assurance—in the form of content generation, expert review, copyediting and printing time—may have made this slow, expensive and exclusionary approach inevitable. However, AI is changing everything.

This series is very different; it is created by AI. The cover of each volume identifies the work as "created under the supervision of" an expert in the field. However, that person is not an author in the traditional sense. The creator of each volume has been trained by the DTL staff in the use of AI and *the creator has used AI to create, edit, revise and recreate the text that you see*. With that creation process clearly identified, let me explain the goals of this series.

Our Goals:

Credibility: Although AI has made—and continues to make—huge strides over the last few years, no unsupervised AI can create a truly reliable or fully credible college or seminary level text. The limitations of AI generated content sometimes originates from the limitations of the content itself (the training set may be inadequate), but more often, user dissatisfaction with AI-generated content arises from human errors associated with poor prompt engineering. The DTL Press has sought to overcome both of these problems by hiring established scholars with widely recognized expertise to create books within their areas of expertise and by training those scholars and experts in AI prompt engineering. To be clear, the scholar whose name appears on the cover of this work has created this volume—generating, reading, regenerating, rereading and revising the work. Even though the work was generated (in varying degrees) by AI, the names of our scholarly creators appear on the cover as a guarantee that the content is equally credible with any introductory work which that scholar/creator would pen using the traditional model.

Affordability: The DTL Press is committed to the idea that affordability should not be a barrier to knowledge. *All persons are equally deserving of the right to know and to understand.* Therefore, ebook versions of all DTL Press books are available from the DTL libraries without charge, and available as print books for a nominal fee. Our scholar/creators are to be thanked for their willingness to forego traditional royalty arrangements. (Our creators are compensated for their generative work, but they do not receive royalties in the traditional sense.)

Accessibility: The DTL Press would like to make high quality, low cost introductory textbooks available to everyone, everywhere in the world. The books in this series are immediately made available in multiple languages. The DTL Press will create translations in other languages upon request. Translations are, of course, generated by AI.

Our Acknowledged Limitations:

Some readers are undoubtedly thinking, "but AI can only produce derivative scholarship; AI can't create original, innovative scholarship." That criticism is, of course, largely accurate. AI is largely limited to aggregating, organizing and repackaging pre-existing ideas (although sometimes in ways that can be used to accelerate and refine the production of original scholarship). Still while acknowledging this inherent limitation of AI, the DTL Press would offer two comments: (1) Introductory texts are seldom meant to be truly ground breaking in their originality and (2) the DTL Press has other series dedicated to publishing original scholarship with traditional authorship.

Our Invitation:

The DTL Press would like to fundamentally reshape academic publishing in the theological world to make scholarship more accessible and more affordable in two ways. First, we would like to generate introductory texts in all areas of theological discourse, so that no one is ever forced to "buy a textbook" in any language. It is our vision for professors anywhere to be able to use one book, two books or an entire set of books in this series as the *introductory* textbooks for their classes. Second, we would also like to publish traditionally authored scholarly monographs for Open Access (free) distribution for an advanced scholarly readership.

Finally, the DTL Press is non-confessional and will publish works in any area of religious studies. Traditionally authored books are peer-reviewed; AI-generated introductory book creation is open to anyone with the required expertise to supervise content generation in that area of discourse. If you share the DTL Press's commitment to credibility, affordability and accessibility, contact us about changing the world of theological publishing by contributing to this series or a more traditionally authored series.

With high expectations,
Thomas E. Phillips
DTL Press Executive Director
www.thedtl.org

Chapter 1
The Nature and Scope of the Synoptic Gospels

What Are the Synoptic Gospels?

The first three books of the New Testament — Matthew, Mark, and Luke — are commonly referred to as the synoptic gospels, a term derived from the Greek words *syn* ("together") and *opsis* ("view"). The term points to the fact that these Gospels share a common perspective and can be "seen together" in terms of content, structure, and even wording. Scholars often use a tool called a *synopsis* to place these Gospels side by side in parallel columns, making it easier to observe the overlaps and discrepancies between them. For example, one can compare how all three Gospels tell the story of Jesus' baptism by John the Baptist. The wording and sequence are remarkably similar, but there are also telling differences in emphasis and tone.

This shared material includes not only narratives of Jesus' public ministry — his miracles, teachings, and confrontations with authorities — but also his crucifixion and resurrection. Yet these Gospels are not mere copies of one another. Each one has its own distinctive voice and theological purpose. Mark, believed by many to be the earliest, is fast-paced and dramatic, portraying Jesus as a suffering Messiah who is misunderstood and rejected. Matthew reuses much of Mark's material but adapts it to highlight Jesus as a teacher and fulfillment of Jewish prophecy. It includes lengthy teaching sections like the Sermon on the Mount, linking Jesus closely with figures like Moses and David. Luke, the longest of the three, presents a wide-angle view of Jesus' ministry, giving special attention to marginalized groups — women, the poor, Gentiles — and emphasizing themes of divine compassion and universal salvation.

Recognizing both the similarities and differences among the Synoptic Gospels raises foundational questions: Why are these texts so alike? How do we explain their differences? What do these literary relationships tell us about early followers of Jesus and how they shaped and passed on his story? These are not just historical curiosities; they affect how we understand the Gospels' portrayal of Jesus, the message he proclaimed, and the significance that early communities attached to his life and death.

Equally important is the recognition that these Gospels are not neutral historical reports or modern biographies. Rather, they are theological narratives — crafted compositions designed to bear witness to the meaning of Jesus' life, not just to its events. The Evangelists, or Gospel writers, selected and arranged material to communicate convictions about who Jesus was and what his message meant for their communities. They were not passive transmitters of information but active interpreters and narrators. Understanding the Gospels as theological narratives helps us read them not just for what "happened," but for what the authors believed mattered most.

This perspective has been emphasized by numerous scholars, such as Luke Timothy Johnson, who writes in *The Writings of the New Testament* that the Gospels are "witness documents," written to inspire faith and shape identity, not simply to record facts. Similarly, Marianne Meye Thompson, in *The Promise of the Father*, reminds readers that the Gospels are embedded in the theological concerns of their time — each responding to specific challenges, questions, and hopes within early Jesus-following communities.

Reading the Gospels thoughtfully requires attentiveness to these narrative dynamics and to the deep convictions that animate each text.

Why Are the Synoptic Gospels Important?

The Synoptic Gospels have shaped Christian identity, theology, and practice for nearly two millennia. But beyond their central role in religious life, they are also essential sources for anyone who seeks to understand the historical Jesus, the formation of early Christian communities, and the social and political world of first-century Judea and Galilee. These Gospels provide layered portraits of Jesus as teacher, prophet, healer, and Messiah, and they preserve a rich diversity of responses to his message and mission.

One reason the Synoptic Gospels matter so much is that they offer complementary windows into Jesus' life and legacy. No single Gospel tells the "whole story." Instead, each one offers a theological interpretation, shaped by particular community concerns, literary strategies, and scriptural understandings. For example, Matthew's Gospel contains numerous citations of the Hebrew Scriptures to show that Jesus fulfills Jewish prophecy, while Luke begins with a sweeping historical introduction and continues the story in a second volume, the Acts of the Apostles.

Because the Gospels are not eyewitness diaries or journalistic accounts, thoughtful readers must ask: What do these stories mean in the context of their telling? How do they reflect both memory and meaning? These questions have led scholars to develop different methods of interpretation — historical, literary, narrative, redactional — all designed to help readers grasp how the Gospels communicate.

For instance, James D. G. Dunn emphasizes the "oral tradition" behind the written Gospels in his work

Jesus Remembered, arguing that the stories about Jesus circulated in living communities long before they were written down. Others, such as Sandra Schneiders, draw on literary and hermeneutical methods to understand the Gospels as texts that both reflect and shape belief. This diversity of approach illustrates the richness of Gospel study — it is not confined to one angle but invites interdisciplinary insight.

Similarities and Differences: Setting Up the Synoptic Problem

One of the most enduring and influential scholarly questions surrounding the Synoptic Gospels is known as the Synoptic Problem. This term refers to the puzzle of how to account for both the similarities and differences among Matthew, Mark, and Luke. For example, over 90% of Mark's content is found in Matthew, and about 50% of it appears in Luke. Yet Matthew and Luke also contain material not found in Mark — such as the Lord's Prayer, the Beatitudes, and several unique parables — which raises questions about how these texts were composed and whether they shared common written or oral sources.

The most widely accepted solution today is the Two-Source Hypothesis, which proposes that Mark was written first, and that both Matthew and Luke used Mark as a source. In addition, Matthew and Luke are thought to have drawn on a now-lost document called Q — a hypothetical collection of Jesus' sayings, such as the instructions to love enemies and the warnings against hypocrisy. While Q has never been discovered in manuscript form, its theoretical existence helps explain how Matthew and Luke share certain material absent from Mark.

Not all scholars accept the Q theory. The Farrer Hypothesis, for example, argues that Luke used both

Mark and Matthew directly, eliminating the need for Q. Proponents such as Mark Goodacre in *The Case against Q* find this model more economical and supported by literary evidence. Meanwhile, other scholars, like John Kloppenborg, continue to defend the Q hypothesis and reconstruct its likely contents and theological themes in works such as *Exavacating Q*.

Debates over the Synoptic Problem may seem technical at first, but they matter deeply. They affect how we understand the formation of the Gospels, the transmission of Jesus' teachings, and the editorial strategies employed by the Evangelists. Was there a common source that emphasized Jesus' ethical sayings and apocalyptic warnings? Did Luke deliberately adjust Matthew's order and content, or did he have access to independent traditions? Engaging with these questions opens the door to understanding how early Jesus-followers grappled with his memory and message in diverse contexts.

How Should We Read the Synoptic Gospels?

Reading the Synoptic Gospels thoughtfully requires more than simply absorbing their content. It involves careful attention to the form, structure, language, and theological vision of each Gospel. These texts are not only records of past events; they are crafted narratives designed to shape the beliefs and practices of those who read them. As such, readers are invited to pay attention to what each Gospel emphasizes, how it structures the story of Jesus, and what theological messages it conveys.

For example, the Gospel of Mark repeatedly portrays Jesus instructing people not to reveal his identity—the so-called Messianic Secret. Why does Mark present Jesus this way? Is it to emphasize the mysterious nature of Jesus' role, or to reflect the misunderstanding of the disciples? In contrast, Matthew places strong emphasis on Jesus as teacher, presenting long discourses like the Sermon on the Mount that structure his ethical vision. Luke, for its part, places women, foreigners, and the poor at the center of the Gospel story, drawing out themes of inclusion, justice, and divine mercy.

Scholars such as Elizabeth Struthers Malbon, using narrative criticism, explore how stories are told — not just what is told. In *Mark's Jesus*, Malbon shows how Mark's portrayal of Jesus is shaped through literary techniques like irony, narrative gaps, and ambiguity. Similarly, Joel Green has argued that Luke's theology is embedded in the way stories unfold over time, and that we must trace narrative development — not just theological propositions.

Thus, reading the Synoptic Gospels carefully involves asking questions like: What do the choices of the Evangelist reveal about their community? How are characters portrayed? What narrative patterns emerge? What is left unsaid, and why might that matter? Such reading is a rich, layered process — one that rewards curiosity and sustained engagement.

What Is the Purpose of Thoughtful Study of the Synoptic Gospels?

Engaging the Synoptic Gospels thoughtfully means approaching them with seriousness, curiosity, and a willingness to learn — not only about Jesus but also about the communities that followed him, the world they inhabited, and the literary forms they used to express their faith. It involves studying the Gospels not simply to affirm preexisting beliefs, but to explore their depth, diversity, and theological artistry.

This kind of study does not require abandoning personal conviction; rather, it invites readers into deeper reflection. Just as one can study a great work of art or music with both emotional appreciation and technical insight, so too the Gospels can be studied for their meaning, complexity, and enduring impact. As we read with care, we begin to see how these texts have shaped the moral imagination, religious thought, and communal life of countless generations.

In this spirit, thoughtful study brings together insights from multiple disciplines — history, theology, literature, cultural studies — to help us understand the Gospels more fully. Scholars like Dale C. Allison Jr., N. T. Wright, and Amy-Jill Levine have each contributed to this broader conversation. Allison emphasizes the layers of memory and meaning in Jesus traditions (*Constructing Jesus*), Wright situates the Gospels in the political world of Second Temple Judaism (*Jesus and the Victory of God*), and Levine challenges readers to hear the Gospels with fresh ears, sensitive to their Jewish roots and modern implications (*Short Stories by Jesus*).

Ultimately, the Synoptic Gospels are not just ancient texts; they are living narratives that continue to shape ethical, spiritual, and communal life. To study them thoughtfully is to listen carefully, to ask questions boldly, and to embrace the richness of a tradition that remains vibrant and transformative.

Chapter 2
The Synoptic Problem

Revisiting the Puzzle: A Deeper Look

In Chapter 1, we introduced the Synoptic Problem — the term scholars use to describe the literary relationships among the Gospels of Matthew, Mark, and Luke. There, we noted that these three texts are strikingly similar in content and wording, often telling the same stories in the same sequence, and sometimes using the very same phrases. Yet they also differ — sometimes subtly, sometimes dramatically — in what they include, what they leave out, how they arrange material, and how they portray Jesus and his mission. The question at the heart of the Synoptic Problem is: How do we account for both the similarities and the differences among these three Gospels?

This is not simply an abstract or technical concern. To understand how these Gospels were composed is to better understand the nature of Gospel writing, the processes of memory and tradition in the early Jesus movement, and the distinctive theological perspectives that shaped the story of Jesus in different communities. By examining the Synoptic Problem more fully, we uncover not just how the Gospels relate to each other, but how the early followers of Jesus shaped and passed on his story in diverse, yet interconnected, ways.

The Evidence of Similarity and Difference

Careful readers of the Gospels soon notice that Matthew, Mark, and Luke share a great deal of content. These shared sections — often called the "triple tradition" — include core episodes such as Jesus' baptism, his temptation in the wilderness, the calling of the disciples, the feeding of the five thousand, and the events of the Passion. In many of these stories, the wording is nearly identical across the Gospels, down to sentence structure and vocabulary. This suggests not just common memory or oral tradition, but direct literary borrowing — that is, one or more authors were using another Gospel as a written source.

Yet alongside these similarities are equally important differences. Each Gospel has its own unique material. Matthew includes an extended birth narrative, the visit of the magi, the Sermon on the Mount, and the parable of the sheep and the goats — none of which appear in Mark or Luke. Luke includes a different birth story, featuring shepherds, angels, and the Magnificat, along with parables like the Good Samaritan and the Prodigal Son. Mark, for its part, is the shortest and starkest of the three, often omitting material that Matthew and Luke include. It also has a distinctive narrative style, moving quickly from one event to another with the word "immediately," and often portrays the disciples in a less flattering light.

Perhaps even more telling are the differences in theological tone and emphasis. Mark's Jesus is secretive about his identity and often misunderstood, while Matthew's Jesus is a master teacher who speaks in five major discourses, echoing Moses and the Torah. Luke's Jesus is compassionate, attentive to women and outsiders, and filled with the Spirit of God from the beginning. These distinctive features point to deliberate choices by the Gospel writers — choices that reflect both theological aims and literary craftsmanship.

The Two-Source Hypothesis: A Widespread Scholarly Model

The Two-Source Hypothesis (2SH) is the most widely accepted theory for explaining the literary relationship among the Synoptic Gospels. It maintains that Mark was the first Gospel written, and that Matthew and Luke independently used Mark as a source. In addition to Mark, Matthew and Luke are also believed to have had access to another written source, now lost, which scholars refer to as Q. This two-source model offers a coherent explanation for both the material shared by all three Synoptic Gospels and the material found in Matthew and Luke but not in Mark.

This theory developed over time. It gained its classical formulation in the early twentieth century through the work of B. H. Streeter, who proposed not only Mark and Q but also material unique to Matthew (which he called M) and material unique to Luke (L). Although later scholarship has placed less emphasis on M and L as discrete documents, Streeter's basic insight remains central: Matthew and Luke each drew on multiple sources, combining and adapting them to fit their own theological and literary aims.

The heart of the Two-Source Hypothesis lies in its explanation of double tradition material — passages found in both Matthew and Luke but absent from Mark. These include some of Jesus' most familiar teachings, such as the Lord's Prayer, the Sermon on the Plain (Luke's parallel to Matthew's Sermon on the Mount), ethical sayings like "love your enemies," and parables such as the lost sheep. The consistency of this material, along with the often high level of verbal agreement between Matthew and Luke in these passages, suggests that both drew from a common textual source.

The hypothetical document Q, while not preserved in any manuscript, is thought to have been a sayings gospel—a collection of Jesus' teachings without narrative framing. Scholars such as John S. Kloppenborg have made significant contributions to the study of Q. In *The Formation of Q*, Kloppenborg identifies two major layers in the text: an earlier "sapiential" layer focused on wisdom teachings (e.g., blessings and ethical instructions), and a later "apocalyptic" layer warning of judgment and emphasizing the urgency of repentance. This layered view of Q reflects the dynamism of early Christian theology, shaped over time by differing communal needs and concerns.

Belief in the existence of Q also reflects assumptions about the independence of Matthew and Luke. If they did not know each other's Gospels, then their agreement in non-Markan material must be due to another common source. Supporters of the Two-Source Hypothesis find this explanation more plausible than the idea of direct literary dependence between Matthew and Luke, especially given the degree to which they diverge in ordering, expanding, or locating this shared material.

While Q remains a hypothetical construct, the Two-Source Hypothesis continues to provide a powerful framework for exploring the literary interconnections among the Gospels, while also allowing for their diversity of style, content, and theological emphasis.

Markan Priority: Why Mark Probably Came First

The idea that Mark was the earliest of the Synoptic Gospels—known as Markan Priority—is foundational to most modern theories of Gospel origins, including the Two-Source Hypothesis. This position is not only widely held but supported by several compelling lines of internal and external evidence.

First, Mark's Gospel is significantly shorter than either Matthew or Luke, and much of its content appears — often verbatim — in the other two. Matthew contains roughly 90% of Mark, and Luke includes more than half. When Matthew and Luke both include Markan material, they frequently agree with each other, sometimes preserving Mark's wording almost exactly. This pattern strongly suggests that Mark was used as a source document.

Second, Mark's language and style are generally more primitive or less refined than those of Matthew and Luke. Mark's Greek is unpolished and full of colloquialisms, redundancies, and vivid but awkward expressions. For instance, Mark often uses the word immediately (Greek: *euthus*) to transition rapidly from one scene to the next, giving the narrative a breathless and dramatic pace. Matthew and Luke frequently smooth out these rough edges, eliminating redundancies and substituting more elegant constructions. This pattern of linguistic improvement suggests that Mark's version came first and was later revised by the other Evangelists.

Third, Mark includes several challenging or problematic details that Matthew and Luke either omit or soften. In Mark 3:21, for example, Jesus' own family tries to restrain him, saying, "He is out of his mind." Neither Matthew nor Luke includes this episode. Similarly, Mark portrays Jesus as limited in power or knowledge in certain scenes, such as when he is unable to perform miracles in his hometown (Mark 6:5) or when he confesses ignorance about the timing of the end (Mark 13:32). These features are often theologically difficult, and it is more likely that later authors would revise or omit them rather than invent them. The editorial logic of improvement runs more plausibly from Mark to Matthew and Luke than the reverse.

Scholars such as Joel Marcus and Adela Yarbro Collins, both of whom have published major commentaries on Mark, emphasize the theological depth and literary sophistication of the Gospel, despite its "rougher" surface. They highlight Mark's apocalyptic urgency, narrative irony, and central emphasis on Jesus as the suffering Son of God. Recognizing Mark as the earliest Gospel helps scholars trace the development of this theological portrait through the more expansive and interpretive renderings in Matthew and Luke.

The theory of Markan Priority not only makes sense of literary patterns, but also underscores how Gospel writers functioned as interpreters and editors, not merely compilers of tradition. By identifying Mark as the foundational Gospel, we begin to see how subsequent Evangelists engaged with earlier material — preserving, reshaping, and recontextualizing it for new audiences.

Alternatives to the Two-Source Theory: Farrer, Griesbach, and Other Models

Although the Two-Source Hypothesis remains dominant, it is not without its detractors. Several alternative theories have been proposed that attempt to solve the Synoptic Problem without recourse to a hypothetical Q document. The most prominent of these is the Farrer Hypothesis, followed by the Griesbach Hypothesis and other less widely accepted models.

The Farrer Hypothesis maintains that Mark was written first, followed by Matthew, and then Luke, who used both of the previous Gospels. This theory eliminates the need for Q entirely, arguing instead that the material common to Matthew and Luke (the so-called "double tradition") can be explained by Luke's direct use of Matthew. This would mean that Luke selected, edited, and reorganized Matthew's content based on his own theological priorities.

Advocates of this view, such as Mark Goodacre, argue that this explanation is more economical and better supported by the literary evidence than postulating a lost source. Goodacre's work, including *The Case Against Q*, challenges the assumptions behind the Two-Source model and argues that Luke's literary techniques—his omissions, relocations, and reinterpretations of Matthew's material—make more sense if he had access to Matthew's text.

The Farrer model also draws support from patterns of verbal agreement between Matthew and Luke. In some passages, the agreement is so close that it is difficult to explain apart from direct literary dependence. Yet the Farrer Hypothesis is not without difficulties. For example, if Luke used Matthew, why would he omit large and theologically rich sections such as most of the Sermon on the Mount? Why does Luke so thoroughly rearrange or recontextualize Matthew's material, even to the point of obscuring its structure? These editorial choices raise questions that scholars continue to debate.

The Griesbach Hypothesis, or Two-Gospel Hypothesis, proposes a different order altogether: that Matthew was written first, followed by Luke, and then Mark, who used both earlier Gospels to create a condensed and streamlined narrative. This model, revived by William R. Farmer in the twentieth century, argues for the primacy of Matthew and sees Luke and Mark as successive reworkings of that original Gospel. Griesbach supporters point to early Christian tradition that names Matthew as the first Gospel and emphasize the theological coherence of Luke as dependent on Matthew.

Yet this view has faced significant challenges. If Mark had access to both Matthew and Luke, why would he omit extensive material — including the birth narratives, key teachings, and parables — and present a more abrupt and less developed account? Why would a later writer produce a shorter and seemingly less comprehensive Gospel by leaving out so much from two fuller ones? These questions have led most scholars to conclude that the direction of dependence runs the other way: from Mark to Matthew and Luke.

Other models, such as theories involving multiple oral traditions, lost early Gospel-like texts, or complex redactional layers, have also been proposed. These reflect the intricate and dynamic nature of Gospel composition. Regardless of the specific model adopted, all scholars agree on the importance of reading the Gospels as products of deliberate shaping — not as spontaneous transcripts of events but as narratives forged in communities, formed by tradition, and guided by theological vision.

Why the Synoptic Problem Matters

To engage the Synoptic Problem is to confront some of the deepest and most formative questions in Gospel studies. Understanding how the Synoptic Gospels were written and how they relate to one another helps readers make sense of both their agreements and their differences. It sheds light on the editorial strategies of the Evangelists, the ways in which oral and written traditions were preserved, and the theological priorities that shaped each Gospel narrative.

The Synoptic Problem also has major implications for our understanding of the historical Jesus. If we can determine which sources are earliest and how they were used, we can better assess which teachings and actions of Jesus may go back to the earliest memories of his followers. Scholars like James D. G. Dunn, in *Jesus Remembered*, have emphasized the importance of oral tradition and communal memory in shaping the Gospels, while others such as Dale C. Allison Jr. and E. P. Sanders have tried to distinguish the probable historical core from later theological interpretation.

Moreover, the Synoptic Problem invites us to think carefully about the nature of Scripture itself. The Gospels are not identical accounts dictated from heaven, but diverse and dynamic testimonies shaped by different communities for different purposes. This diversity does not weaken their message but enriches it. It reminds us that the truth of Jesus is not confined to a single perspective but is woven through multiple witnesses, each with its own emphasis and voice.

Looking Ahead: Reading the Synoptics with Insight

As we move forward in our study of the Synoptic Gospels, we carry with us the insights gained from wrestling with the Synoptic Problem. We now recognize that these texts are interconnected yet distinctive, shaped by both shared tradition and individual theology. We understand that each Gospel is part of a larger literary conversation, and that appreciating their similarities and differences allows us to hear their message more clearly.

Rather than reducing the Gospels to mechanical compositions or historical puzzles, this kind of study opens us to their depth, richness, and theological power. It enables us to read with greater care, to ask better questions, and to appreciate the complexity of early Christian witness. The Synoptic Problem, then, is not simply a difficulty to be solved — it is a gateway to deeper understanding, inviting us to see the Gospels as layered, purposeful, and alive with meaning.

Chapter 3
Historical and Cultural Context of the Gospels

Introduction: Why Context Matters

When we read the Synoptic Gospels — Matthew, Mark, and Luke — we enter into narratives filled with compelling characters, urgent proclamations, and vivid moments of divine encounter. But these stories, powerful as they are, did not emerge in isolation. They were written within a complex web of historical circumstances, cultural traditions, political pressures, and religious expectations. To understand them well, and to hear their message as their original audiences might have, we must enter into the world behind the text — the concrete realities of first-century life in the eastern Mediterranean.

Context does not replace meaning — it illuminates it. The more we understand about Roman imperial rule, Jewish sectarianism, popular messianic hopes, economic structures, and Greco-Roman thought, the more clearly we can hear the theological, ethical, and political claims of the Gospels. In fact, many of Jesus' actions and teachings are only fully intelligible when we understand the environment in which they were proclaimed: a world of imperial power and peasant struggle, of synagogue worship and temple sacrifice, of hopeful apocalyptic longing and grinding economic hardship.

This chapter explores the historical and cultural matrix of the Synoptic Gospels by focusing on five interrelated dimensions: the Roman imperial context, the diverse expressions of first-century Judaism, the apocalyptic worldview and eschatological hopes that permeated Jewish life, the destruction of the Temple in 70 CE, and the pervasive influence of Greco-Roman culture. By attending to these forces, we come to appreciate not only what the Gospels say, but why they say it the way they do—and how that message might have functioned for their earliest audiences.

The Roman Imperial Context

At the time the Gospels were written—roughly between 65 and 90 CE—the Roman Empire was the dominant political and military power across the Mediterranean world. Roman rule over Judea and Galilee had begun in 63 BCE, when Pompey annexed the region, and it remained firmly in place through a combination of military might, economic extraction, and ideological persuasion. The Romans did not merely govern through force; they built a political theology, a set of stories and symbols that portrayed the emperor as the bringer of divine peace and order.

This imperial ideology permeated public life. The emperor was not only ruler but was often regarded as divine. Titles such as "Son of God," "Savior," "Lord," and "bringer of peace" (Latin: *DIVI FILIUS, SOTER, KYRIOS, PAX ROMANA*) were routinely applied to emperors like Augustus. These titles were emblazoned on coins, inscribed in temples, and chanted in public rituals. Roman rule was not simply a political arrangement—it was a sacred order, and loyalty to Caesar was both civic and religious.

In this context, the proclamation that Jesus is "Lord" (*kyrios*) was not just a spiritual claim. It was a counter-imperial assertion, a declaration that true authority and salvation resided not in Caesar but in the crucified and risen Christ. Scholars such as Richard Horsley, in *Jesus and Empire*, and Tom Wright, in *Paul and the Faithfulness of God*, have highlighted how early

Christian language subverted Roman power by using its very vocabulary in new and radical ways.

Economically, the effects of Roman imperialism were deeply felt. Heavy taxation funded Roman roads, armies, and elite lifestyles. Local rulers, such as the Herods, collected taxes on Rome's behalf, often enriching themselves in the process. Land was increasingly concentrated in the hands of a few, while peasant farmers, day laborers, and artisans struggled to survive. The Gospels' frequent attention to debt, hunger, injustice, and wealth is not abstract moralizing—it reflects a real and oppressive economic reality.

When Jesus speaks of the kingdom of God, shares meals with the poor, or warns about the dangers of wealth, he does so in a world where power and money were controlled by a small elite. When he heals the sick or touches the untouchable, he challenges not only religious purity laws but also the social hierarchies enforced by imperial and local power structures. To read the Gospels without this imperial background is to miss much of their radical edge and their vision of a new kind of community rooted in divine justice rather than imperial control.

Jewish Diversity in the First Century

First-century Judaism was marked by remarkable internal diversity. Far from being a monolithic religion, Judaism at the time of Jesus included multiple groups, movements, and perspectives, each interpreting the Scriptures and envisioning Israel's future in different ways. These differences help us understand the conflicts in the Gospels—not as rejections of Judaism per se, but as part of an internal Jewish debate about how to be faithful to God in a time of oppression and uncertainty.

21

Among the most well-known groups were the Pharisees, who emphasized Torah observance, belief in the resurrection of the dead, and the authority of both the written and oral law. They were respected for their scholarship and religious devotion, and they held significant influence in synagogues, which were the local centers of Jewish community life. The Gospels often portray Jesus in conflict with the Pharisees, especially over issues like purity, Sabbath observance, and the interpretation of the law. But these disputes should be seen as intra-Jewish arguments, reflecting divergent visions of covenant faithfulness.

The Sadducees, in contrast, were associated with the Temple priesthood and the Jerusalem elite. They denied the resurrection and the oral law and were often seen as more cooperative with Roman authorities. Their power was rooted in the Temple system, which was central to Jewish religious life until its destruction in 70 CE. The Gospels present the Sadducees as opponents of Jesus, especially in matters concerning resurrection and religious authority.

A third group, the Essenes, likely connected to the community at Qumran (known from the Dead Sea Scrolls), withdrew from society and formed a separatist, apocalyptic movement. They anticipated an imminent divine intervention to purify Israel and establish a righteous remnant. Their writings speak of two messianic figures—one priestly and one royal—and a final battle between the "Sons of Light" and the "Sons of Darkness." While not mentioned in the Gospels, their worldview echoes aspects of John the Baptist's message and helps contextualize the apocalyptic themes in Jesus' teaching.

Beyond these groups, there were also popular messianic movements and revolutionary figures, such as Judas the Galilean, who resisted Roman taxation and authority. These figures were often seen as threats to the status quo and were quickly crushed by Roman power. In this environment, the hope for a messiah—a divinely anointed leader who would restore Israel's fortunes—remained a powerful and dangerous expectation.

At the heart of Jewish daily life were practices of prayer, almsgiving, purity, and Sabbath observance. Most Jews did not belong to sectarian groups but expressed their faith through synagogue worship, pilgrimage festivals (such as Passover), and the rhythms of Torah-based piety. The Gospels assume this world: Jesus teaches in synagogues, attends festivals, and engages in debates over purity and law.

Understanding this diverse Jewish landscape is essential for interpreting Jesus' actions. His conflicts with the Pharisees and Sadducees were not anti-Jewish but were part of a broader conversation about what it meant to be Israel, how to interpret God's will, and how to live in a world marked by oppression and longing for redemption.

Apocalyptic Worldview and Eschatological Hope

A significant portion of the Jewish population in the first century lived with a profound sense of unfulfilled promise. Although they believed in the God who had delivered Israel in the past—from Egypt, through exile, and into restoration—they now found themselves under Roman domination, without a Davidic king, and with prophetic silence stretching over centuries. In this setting, many turned to an apocalyptic worldview, a lens through which they could make sense of suffering and injustice while holding on to hope.

Apocalypticism was both a literary genre and a theological orientation. Its key features included dualism—the belief that history is divided between this present evil age and the age to come; revelation—

usually mediated through visions, dreams, or angelic figures; symbolism — often elaborate and cosmic in scope; and a hope for divine intervention, often associated with a final judgment, resurrection of the dead, and the vindication of the righteous. Foundational apocalyptic texts include Daniel, especially chapter 7 with its vision of the "Son of Man," and 1 Enoch, which greatly influenced the worldview of groups like the Essenes.

In the Gospels, these themes surface frequently. Jesus' use of the phrase "kingdom of God" evokes not just general ideas of divine rule, but a dramatic inbreaking of God's justice into a broken world. His parables often speak of a delayed reckoning, a final harvest, or a surprise reversal of fortunes — all staples of apocalyptic thought. Mark 13, often called the "Little Apocalypse," portrays cosmic signs, tribulations, and the coming of the Son of Man — a direct echo of Daniel.

Many modern scholars have emphasized this apocalyptic dimension. Bart Ehrman, in *Jesus: Apocalyptic Prophet of the New Millennium,* argues that Jesus saw himself as a prophet announcing the imminent arrival of God's reign. Dale Allison, in *Constructing Jesus,* builds on this claim, suggesting that Jesus' teaching and symbolic actions — especially his healings and exorcisms — point to a prophetic imagination shaped by a belief in the collapse of the current age and the dawn of a new one.

This apocalyptic hope was not escapist. Rather, it provided moral vision and communal courage. It called people to faithfulness in the present, sustained by the belief that God's justice would ultimately prevail. For many Jews and early followers of Jesus, apocalypticism offered a language of protest and perseverance, affirming that God saw their suffering, that evil would be judged, and that the righteous would be restored. It also framed Jesus' mission not simply as ethical reform but as the inauguration of a new cosmic reality.

The Destruction of the Temple and Its Aftermath

Few events shaped the world of the Gospels and early Christianity as profoundly as the destruction of the Second Temple in Jerusalem by the Romans in 70 CE. This cataclysmic event followed a Jewish revolt that began in 66 CE and was met with overwhelming Roman force. After a brutal siege, the Romans entered the city, destroyed the Temple, and slaughtered or enslaved tens of thousands of its inhabitants. The historian Josephus, a Jewish commander turned Roman chronicler, provides vivid — if sometimes propagandistic — accounts of the war's devastation.

Theologically and culturally, the loss of the Temple was shattering. The Temple was not merely a religious building; it was the center of Jewish identity and worship. It was where sacrifices were offered, where the priesthood ministered, and where heaven and earth were believed to meet. Its destruction called into question the status of the priesthood, the efficacy of atonement, and the future of Jewish life.

For the early Jesus-following communities, the destruction of the Temple was both trauma and theological opportunity. Many scholars believe that the Gospel of Mark, the earliest of the Synoptics, was written shortly before or after this event. In Mark 13, Jesus predicts the Temple's fall, framing it as a divine judgment and urging watchfulness. For these early communities, the Temple's destruction was seen not as the end of hope, but as confirmation of Jesus' prophetic message and the beginning of a new era.

The aftermath of 70 CE also marked a crucial turning point in Jewish history. With the priestly class devastated and the sacrificial system no longer viable, Jewish life began to reorganize around the synagogue, Torah study, and rabbinic leadership. This process gave rise to what we now call Rabbinic Judaism, with its emphasis on ethical conduct, prayer, and communal memory.

For Christians, especially Gentile believers, the event likely accelerated the distancing between synagogue and church. Tensions that had existed between Jesus-followers and other Jewish groups were intensified by trauma, competition, and divergent responses to the crisis. The Gospels — especially Matthew, which preserves some of the sharpest polemic — reflect this period of theological struggle and emerging identity.

At the same time, the destruction of the Temple inspired deep theological reflection. Without a central cultic location, where was God to be found? Could Jesus himself be seen as the new temple, the locus of God's presence? The Gospels implicitly answer this with a resounding yes. The narrative focus on Jesus as the one in whom God dwells, the one who is crucified and raised, becomes the new foundation for understanding atonement, access to God, and divine presence.

Greco-Roman Cultural Influences

While Roman political power and Jewish religious life form the most immediate context of the Gospels, the broader Greco-Roman cultural world must also be considered. Since the conquests of Alexander the Great in the 4th century BCE, Greek language and culture had permeated the eastern Mediterranean. By the first century CE, the region was a mosaic of Hellenistic cities, Greek education, Roman law, and a blend of philosophical and religious traditions.

Most Jews in the eastern Mediterranean were bilingual or trilingual, speaking Aramaic and reading Hebrew Scriptures, but also engaging with Greek as the lingua franca of trade, administration, and intellectual life. The New Testament itself is written in Koine Greek, the everyday dialect used across the Roman world. This enabled the Gospels to circulate widely among both Jewish and Gentile audiences.

Greek education emphasized rhetoric and storytelling, and these influences are visible in the Gospels. The use of parables, symbolic action, structured speeches, and chiastic patterns reflects familiarity with broader literary conventions. Luke, in particular, opens his Gospel with a preface in the style of Greco-Roman historiography (Luke 1:1–4), suggesting that he saw himself not only as a theologian but as a historian addressing a literate audience.

Philosophically, the world of the Gospels was shaped by currents such as Stoicism, Platonism, and popular ethics that emphasized virtue, fate, and the search for divine truth. While the Gospels do not engage these systems explicitly, they do address questions of the good life, human destiny, and the nature of true wisdom. Jesus' teachings about humility, peacemaking, and non-retaliation often run counter to both Roman honor codes and Greco-Roman philosophical ideals.

Religiously, the first-century world was marked by pluralism and syncretism. People worshiped local gods, imperial figures, and deities from mystery religions such as Isis, Mithras, and Dionysus. Sacrifices, rituals, and festivals were woven into the fabric of civic life. Against this background, the early Christian claim that Jesus alone is Lord, and that allegiance to him might require rejecting other loyalties, was both compelling and controversial.

Cities like Antioch, Corinth, Ephesus, and Rome became centers of Christian mission and Gospel reception. Urban life, with its networks of trade, communication, and social diversity, provided fertile ground for the expansion of the Jesus movement. The Gospels themselves may have been composed in or for urban communities navigating how to live faithfully in a complex, multicultural world.

In sum, the Gospels reflect a profound engagement with both Jewish tradition and Greco-Roman culture. They are not provincial or isolated texts but theologically rich documents written in dialogue with empires, philosophies, and social worlds far beyond the hills of Galilee.

Conclusion: Seeing the Gospels in Their World

To approach the Synoptic Gospels with care and insight requires more than reading them as timeless truths or isolated stories. It calls us to situate them within the world that produced them — a world shaped by imperial domination, religious longing, economic disparity, and cultural complexity. Far from reducing their meaning, this contextual awareness expands it, helping us to hear the Gospels as their first hearers may have: as good news proclaimed in the midst of power, oppression, and hope.

The Gospels speak of Jesus not as a disembodied spiritual figure, but as a Jewish teacher, prophet, and healer who lived under Roman rule, engaged with his religious tradition, and called people to a new vision of God's reign. His message was grounded in the Scriptures of Israel, addressed to real communities, and formed in response to real struggles. He proclaimed a kingdom that was not Caesar's, a community that included the outcast and poor, and a hope that dared to believe in resurrection beyond death and justice beyond empire.

By understanding the historical and cultural context of the Gospels, we not only interpret them more accurately — we also become more attentive to how they continue to speak into our own contexts of injustice, longing, and transformation. The world of the Gospels may be distant, but its themes are strikingly familiar. Then as now, people long for healing, truth, liberation, and hope. And the story of Jesus, once proclaimed in Galilee and written down by Evangelists in the shadow of empire, continues to offer a word of life for those who have ears to hear.

Chapter 4
Source and Redaction Criticism

Introduction: How the Gospels Took Shape

The Synoptic Gospels — Matthew, Mark, and Luke — are not simply collections of Jesus' sayings or unedited historical accounts. They are carefully crafted theological narratives, written by authors who selected, shaped, and arranged material in order to communicate a particular vision of who Jesus was and what his life, death, and resurrection meant. While they are rooted in memory and tradition, they also reflect the interpretive decisions and editorial voices of their authors.

This chapter introduces two of the most important scholarly methods for exploring how the Gospels were composed: source criticism and redaction criticism. Source criticism investigates the written materials that the Gospel writers likely had at their disposal and how they used them. Redaction criticism, by contrast, focuses on how each Evangelist edited and reworked those sources to express particular theological convictions, pastoral concerns, and literary aims.

Both approaches build on the insight that the Gospels emerged from a complex process of tradition, reflection, and composition. They help readers move beyond questions of simple fact or harmonization, and instead appreciate the Gospels as literary and theological constructions, shaped by historical communities seeking to bear faithful witness to the significance of Jesus.

The Emergence of Source Criticism

The modern study of the Gospels began in earnest during the Enlightenment, when scholars first began to ask systematic historical and literary questions about the Bible. In the eighteenth and nineteenth centuries, thinkers like Johann Jakob Griesbach and Christian Hermann Weisse noticed that the Synoptic Gospels shared large portions of text, often in the same sequence and with identical wording in Greek. These patterns suggested not only oral tradition, but also direct literary borrowing.

As this insight developed, scholars proposed various models to explain the Gospels' literary relationships. The most influential of these became the Two-Source Hypothesis, which posits that Mark was the earliest written Gospel, and that both Matthew and Luke used Mark as a source. In addition to Mark, Matthew and Luke appear to share another body of material — sayings of Jesus, especially — found in both but not in Mark. Scholars believe that this material likely came from another shared source, now lost, which has been named Q, from the German word *Quelle*, meaning "source."

This theory explains several features of the Synoptic Gospels. First, it clarifies why over 90 percent of Mark's content appears in Matthew, and over half appears in Luke — suggesting that both later Evangelists were building on Mark's foundational narrative. Second, it accounts for the so-called "double tradition" — material common to Matthew and Luke but absent from Mark, such as the Beatitudes, the Lord's Prayer, and the parable of the lost sheep. Finally, it makes sense of the distinctive content and arrangement found in each Gospel, which often reflects the unique theological interests of the author.

The Q source, while hypothetical, has been studied extensively through textual reconstruction. Scholars such as John S. Kloppenborg have argued that Q had its own theological structure, possibly developing in stages from sapiential (wisdom-focused) to apocalyptic material. James M. Robinson viewed Q as a full-fledged "sayings Gospel," perhaps representing a stream of early Christianity more focused on Jesus' teachings than on the narrative of his death and resurrection.

Source criticism does not claim to recover original documents or eyewitness reports directly, but it does allow scholars and readers to map out how the Gospel writers drew on earlier sources, reshaping inherited material to serve new purposes. It reveals the Gospels as dialogical texts, part of a living and layered tradition of remembering, interpreting, and proclaiming Jesus' significance.

The Logic and Legacy of the Two-Source Hypothesis

The Two-Source Hypothesis remains the most widely accepted model for explaining the literary relationships among the Synoptic Gospels. It has proven effective in illuminating why Matthew and Luke follow Mark's basic narrative structure, while also including substantial sayings material not found in Mark. According to this model, the authors of Matthew and Luke were each working independently, with access to both Mark's Gospel and to Q, but not to each other's writings.

This view clarifies not only the sequence of events but also the theological patterns in the Gospels. For instance, when we compare the temptation narrative in Matthew and Luke, we find them both drawing from a shared source. Yet they place the final temptation in different locations—Matthew ends on a high mountain, while Luke concludes at the temple in Jerusalem. If they were using the same source independently, their variations suggest theological decisions rather than mutual borrowing.

Despite its strengths, the Two-Source Hypothesis is not without challenges. The most significant is that Q has never been discovered as a document, and no early church father mentions it explicitly. Some scholars, such as Mark Goodacre, argue that it is more plausible to think that Luke used both Mark and Matthew directly, eliminating the need for a lost source. This alternative is known as the Farrer Hypothesis and is discussed in Chapter 2.

Nevertheless, the Q theory continues to hold sway among many scholars because it accounts well for both the shared and divergent features of Matthew and Luke. It also reminds us that early Christianity was not a single, unified movement, but a plurality of voices and traditions, some of which preserved teachings of Jesus long before they were shaped into narrative Gospels.

Redaction Criticism: The Evangelists as Theologians

While source criticism focuses on the preexisting materials the Gospel writers used, redaction criticism attends to how they shaped those materials in the act of writing. This method emerged in the mid-twentieth century as scholars began to recognize the Evangelists not merely as editors or collectors, but as creative theologians and authors, each with a distinct theological voice and narrative vision.

Redaction criticism begins with a simple but profound insight: the differences between the Gospels are not necessarily mistakes or contradictions. They are often intentional and meaningful. Each Gospel writer made decisions about what to include, what to omit, how to organize material, and how to frame it with commentary, transitions, or interpretation. These choices reflect theological convictions as well as the needs and concerns of the communities for whom the Gospels were written.

One of the key insights of redaction criticism is that the Gospel writers used their sources not passively, but selectively and purposefully. For example, when Matthew expands or revises Mark, he often does so to emphasize the fulfillment of Scripture, the authority of Jesus as teacher, or the continuity between Jesus and Israel's story. When Luke reshapes the material, he highlights the role of the Holy Spirit, the inclusion of outsiders, and the theme of joy and divine initiative.

Redaction critics look closely at how each Evangelist or Gospel writer adds introductory comments, framing devices, or concluding summaries. They also examine how stories are placed in new literary contexts that change their impact or meaning. What happens when a parable is moved from one part of the narrative to another? What theological significance emerges when a miracle is followed by a particular teaching or confrontation?

This method also pays close attention to editorial tendencies—consistent patterns that reveal an author's theological priorities. For example, Mark tends to portray the disciples as confused, slow to understand, and frequently mistaken. Matthew softens some of these portrayals, likely to encourage his audience by presenting the disciples as more competent and faithful. Luke, in turn, often emphasizes the disciples' ongoing growth and empowerment by the Spirit, preparing them for leadership in the sequel volume, the Acts of the Apostles.

Redaction criticism helps us ask not just, "What does this text say?" but "Why does it say it this way, here, and now?" It invites us to see the Evangelists as interpreters of tradition, not simply transmitters. It reveals the Gospels as dynamic engagements with memory, Scripture, theology, and the real-life concerns of early Christian communities.

Examples of Redaction at Work

The baptism of Jesus provides a clear window into redactional strategy. In Mark's Gospel, the event is told with brevity and immediacy. Jesus is baptized by John, the heavens are torn open, and a voice declares, "You are my beloved Son." Matthew expands this scene significantly, introducing a dialogue in which John initially resists baptizing Jesus, and Jesus responds, "Let it be so now; for it is proper for us in this way to fulfill all righteousness." This exchange not only defends the act of baptism but also frames it within Matthew's theme of Jesus fulfilling divine purpose and modeling obedience. Luke's account shifts focus again, omitting John's role and emphasizing that the Holy Spirit descends while Jesus is praying, thereby highlighting Luke's broader theme of Spirit-empowered prayer and divine guidance.

The passion predictions in the Synoptic Gospels offer another powerful case. In Mark, Jesus predicts his suffering and death three times, each time followed by a misunderstanding on the part of the disciples, creating a rhythm of prophecy, confusion, and correction. This narrative pattern reinforces Mark's portrayal of discipleship as costly and often misunderstood. Matthew retains these predictions but often clarifies or augments them, linking Jesus' suffering more directly to fulfillment of Scripture and divine intention. Luke, meanwhile, modifies the predictions to emphasize the necessity of Jesus' mission and the prophetic character of his journey to Jerusalem.

Perhaps the most famous redactional moment is the ending of Matthew's Gospel: the Great Commission. Unique to Matthew, this scene presents the risen Jesus sending his disciples into all nations to baptize and teach in his name. It is a fitting climax to a Gospel that has presented Jesus as a new Moses, a teacher of righteousness, and the one in whom Israel's story finds fulfillment. Mark and Luke do not include this scene in the same way; their endings are shaped by different theological and literary aims.

These examples illustrate how redaction criticism allows us to read the Gospels not as rigid histories or doctrinal blueprints but as narrative theologies — texts composed with intention and imagination, inviting readers into a world where divine action, human response, and community identity are inextricably linked.

Conclusion: The Gospels as Interpreted Witness

Source and redaction criticism have transformed the way thoughtful readers approach the Synoptic Gospels. Together, they reveal the layered composition and theological depth of these texts, helping us see the Gospel writers not as stenographers of tradition but as pastoral theologians, shaped by their communities and guided by their convictions.

These methods encourage us to ask deeper questions. Why does Matthew emphasize fulfillment? Why does Mark highlight mystery and misunderstanding? Why does Luke draw attention to the poor, the outsider, and the Spirit's guidance? Such questions are not distractions from faith — they are invitations to encounter the richness of the Gospel traditions more fully.

By attending to sources, we learn how early Christians preserved and transmitted the story of Jesus across time, place, and community. By attending to redaction, we learn how that story was interpreted, reshaped, and re-presented to speak a fresh word to changing contexts. For students, teachers, preachers, and careful readers, these tools offer both challenge and insight, reminding us that the Gospels are not only testimonies of past events, but living texts — crafted with theological intention and continuing to speak into the present.

Chapter 5
Form Criticism and Oral Tradition

Introduction: Remembering Jesus in Community

Before the Gospels were written down, the story of Jesus lived in the spoken words and shared memories of his followers. These early Christians did not initially record what Jesus said or did in writing; instead, they proclaimed, recounted, retold, and interpreted his words and actions in a variety of settings — at meals, in worship, during debates, and while on mission. This period of oral transmission was not a gap in the tradition, but rather a dynamic and formative stage in which the Jesus story was shaped to address the life of the community.

As this oral tradition was eventually gathered and written into the Gospels, the material carried with it distinctive forms — small, self-contained units of story or speech — that scholars later came to identify and study. These forms include miracle stories, pronouncement stories, parables, sayings, and other units that made the Jesus tradition memorable, repeatable, and adaptable. The method of studying these building blocks came to be known as form criticism.

Form criticism, along with related studies of oral tradition and memory, helps us understand how the Gospels were composed, not simply from literary sources but from lived, performed tradition. It allows us to appreciate the texture of the Synoptic Gospels as both historical memory and theological artistry — the result of communities who remembered Jesus in ways that sustained faith, formed identity, and addressed real-life questions.

The Origins and Aims of Form Criticism

Form criticism arose in early twentieth-century German scholarship, especially in the work of Rudolf Bultmann, Martin Dibelius, and Karl Ludwig Schmidt. These scholars were concerned that source criticism, while helpful in identifying textual relationships, did not explain how the Gospel materials originally emerged. Form critics asked: before the Evangelists wrote their Gospels, how were stories about Jesus preserved, passed on, and shaped? What social settings gave rise to specific types of stories or sayings? And how did these forms evolve as they were used in worship, catechesis, or mission?

The fundamental assumption of form criticism is that the Gospels are composed of independent units of tradition—small stories, sayings, or episodes that circulated orally before being compiled into continuous narratives. These units were shaped by the needs and life situations (*Sitz im Leben*) of the early Christian communities, and their form reveals something of their original use.

For example, a short miracle story may have been used in preaching to proclaim Jesus' authority and divine power. A controversy story might have been told to address opposition or clarify ethical boundaries. A parable could have functioned as a teaching tool or a prophetic challenge. By identifying the form and function of these units, form critics hoped to reconstruct the history of the tradition and even get closer to the historical Jesus.

While form criticism has been critiqued—particularly for its speculative reconstructions and its sometimes rigid separation of oral and written stages—

it remains foundational. More recent scholars have built on it by integrating insights from performance theory, social memory studies, and orality studies, all of which affirm that the early Jesus tradition was not fixed in writing but fluid, communal, and shaped through use.

Miracle Stories: Deeds of Power and Signs of Compassion

Among the most vivid and memorable forms in the Synoptic Gospels are miracle stories. These accounts portray Jesus as a man of power and authority — someone who heals the sick, calms the sea, drives out demons, and even raises the dead. These stories are typically brief, dramatic, and structured with a clear beginning, middle, and end.

A typical healing miracle follows a recognizable pattern: a person approaches Jesus (or is brought to him), the condition is described (often in terms of physical suffering or social exclusion), Jesus responds — sometimes with a touch or a word — and the person is healed, with the crowd reacting in awe. Consider the story of the healing of the leper in Mark 1:40–45: the leper begs Jesus for healing, Jesus is moved with compassion, he reaches out and touches the man, pronounces him clean, and then sends him to show himself to the priest. The form is concise but powerful, with emotional depth and theological significance.

Miracle stories functioned in multiple ways. They demonstrated Jesus' authority over illness, nature, spirits, and death. They also signaled the arrival of the kingdom of God — a central theme in Jesus' ministry. These acts of healing and liberation were not just displays of divine power; they were signs of restoration, reversing conditions of impurity, exclusion, or despair. In a world where sickness often meant shame and separation, Jesus' miracles restored individuals to community and dignity.

Form critics categorized these stories into subtypes, including healing miracles, nature miracles, and exorcisms. Each subtype carried its own theological weight. Nature miracles, such as Jesus calming the storm (Mark 4:35–41), evoked Old Testament images of God subduing the sea, suggesting divine identity. Exorcisms, such as the healing of the Gerasene demoniac (Mark 5:1–20), revealed Jesus' power over spiritual evil and his mission to liberate the afflicted, often including those on the margins of Jewish society.

These stories were told and retold because they embodied the hope and promise of the Gospel — that in Jesus, God was at work to heal, liberate, and restore the world.

Pronouncement Stories: Conflict and Clarification

Another widely recognized form is the pronouncement story — a brief narrative that builds toward a climactic saying of Jesus, usually delivered in the context of a challenge, debate, or dramatic moment. These stories were particularly useful for teaching and defending core truths, as they often involved conflict with opponents, such as Pharisees, scribes, or other religious leaders.

The classic example is the story of Jesus' disciples plucking grain on the Sabbath (Mark 2:23–28). The Pharisees question Jesus about this apparent violation of Sabbath law, and Jesus responds by citing Scripture, invoking the example of David, and then declaring, "The Sabbath was made for humankind, and not humankind for the Sabbath; so the Son of Man is lord even of the Sabbath." The entire story is built to lead up to this memorable and authoritative statement, which reorients Sabbath observance around human need and divine authority.

Pronouncement stories typically have four elements: a setting, an occasion of conflict or inquiry, a response from Jesus (usually a saying), and a reaction or resolution. The structure is tight, the dialogue pointed, and the teaching central. They were likely crafted to preserve key teachings of Jesus in ways that were easy to memorize and to repeat in contexts of instruction or controversy.

These stories often illustrate Jesus' wisdom, boldness, and interpretive authority. He challenges established norms, redefines righteousness, and asserts a distinctive understanding of God's will. Whether in disputes over purity laws, Sabbath observance, or forgiveness of sins, pronouncement stories depict Jesus not simply as a healer or prophet, but as a teacher with extraordinary authority—one who speaks on behalf of God and reshapes the moral imagination of his listeners.

Parables and Sayings: Teaching the Kingdom with Imagination and Insight

Among the most beloved and distinctive forms preserved in the Synoptic Gospels are parables—short, imaginative stories that draw on everyday experiences to reveal truths about God, the kingdom, and human life. Jesus' use of parables set him apart as a teacher. Rather than offering abstract theology or rigid commandments, he invited listeners into narratives of surprise, reversal, and reflection.

Parables are not fables or moral tales in the conventional sense. They rarely end with a tidy lesson. Instead, they often contain elements of ambiguity, tension, or shock. Consider the parable of the Good Samaritan (Luke 10:25-37). It begins with a legal question—"Who is my neighbor?"—and ends with a narrative that overturns social expectations. A despised Samaritan becomes the model of mercy, while religious leaders fail to act. The story refuses to define neighbor narrowly and instead calls listeners to reimagine the boundaries of compassion.

Another famous parable, the Prodigal Son (Luke 15:11–32), explores themes of repentance, forgiveness, jealousy, and joy. Its emotional power lies not just in the return of the younger son, but in the unresolved tension with the older brother. Readers are drawn into the story and invited to ask themselves: Where do I stand? What does it mean to welcome others? Can I rejoice when grace is extended?

Form critics noted that many parables follow familiar structures: a simple scenario drawn from daily life, a narrative twist or reversal, and a final moment of judgment or insight. Parables often feature characters and scenarios typical of rural Galilee—farmers, landowners, shepherds, merchants, weddings, and banquets. These local details suggest that the parables originated in Jesus' oral teaching and were well suited for memorization, performance, and adaptation.

In addition to parables, the Gospels also preserve sayings of Jesus that were likely passed down independently of longer narratives. These include aphorisms, proverbs, blessings, and warnings. For example, the sayings "Blessed are the peacemakers" (Matt 5:9), "The last will be first, and the first will be last" (Matt 20:16), and "No one can serve two masters" (Matt 6:24) are brief, vivid, and packed with meaning. Their poetic rhythm and parallelism made them easy to remember and effective for oral transmission.

Many sayings reflect a wisdom tradition, drawing on Hebrew Scriptures and Jewish teaching to articulate a vision of ethical living and divine justice. Others are apocalyptic, pointing to coming judgment, the urgency of repentance, and the dawning of God's kingdom. Still others are countercultural, calling for enemy love, radical generosity, and non-retaliation.

The preservation of these sayings in both Matthew and Luke—often with close verbal agreement—suggests that early communities valued them deeply. Some of these sayings likely came from the hypothesized Q source, while others may have circulated through oral catechesis, especially in house churches and baptismal preparation. Their brevity and forcefulness point to a world in which teachings had to be spoken, heard, and remembered, long before they were written down.

Together, parables and sayings form a vital part of the Gospel tradition. They reflect Jesus' role as a master teacher and storyteller, one who communicated with clarity and depth, drawing people into reflection on God's reign and calling them to transformed lives.

Orality, Memory, and the Life of the Early Church

Form criticism opened the door to a broader conversation about how early Christian communities remembered Jesus and passed on his teaching. In the decades before the Gospels were written, most of what people knew about Jesus came not from scrolls or manuscripts but from community storytelling, public preaching, and ritual performance. This was an oral world, in which stories were heard, recited, adapted, and internalized through repetition and participation.

More recent scholars have extended the insights of form criticism by drawing on oral tradition studies and social memory theory. Thinkers like James D. G. Dunn and Werner Kelber emphasized that oral tradition is not static or fragile. It is both stable and flexible. Core themes—such as Jesus' authority, his compassion, his death and resurrection—remained constant, while details could be adapted to meet the needs of different communities.

Social memory theorists, such as Rafael Rodríguez and Alan Kirk, argue that the process of remembering Jesus was always communal and theological. Communities remembered Jesus not as a neutral historical figure, but as the risen Lord, present through the Spirit and active in the life of the church. The Gospels, then, are not simply historical records but acts of communal memory — reflections on the past shaped by the faith and hope of the present.

This perspective helps explain the diversity within the Gospel tradition. Different communities remembered different sayings, emphasized different aspects of Jesus' ministry, and crafted narratives that spoke to their specific contexts. The forms of tradition — miracle stories, pronouncement stories, parables, and sayings — were not mere leftovers from oral performance; they were the foundation of Christian proclamation, shaped by usage, memory, and theological conviction.

Conclusion: Living Tradition and Faithful Witness

Form criticism and the study of oral tradition remind us that the Gospels are not static texts, dropped from heaven or dictated word-for-word. They are the result of living, faithful communities, remembering, retelling, and reinterpreting the story of Jesus in light of their experience, worship, and mission. Before these traditions were written down, they were preached, sung, prayed, debated, and performed. Their form reflects their function: they were designed to be heard, understood, and passed on.

By attending to the forms in which the Jesus tradition was preserved — miracle stories that inspire awe, pronouncement stories that provoke decision, parables that open the imagination, and sayings that echo with wisdom — we begin to appreciate not only the content of the Gospel, but its communal shape and power. The early church did not merely preserve information about Jesus; it bore witness to him in ways that could be remembered, lived out, and shared.

Form criticism invites us into that process. It helps us hear the Gospels with new ears — not just as readers, but as participants in a tradition that is still unfolding. The stories that once echoed in Galilean hills and house churches continue to shape lives, provoke reflection, and invite faith. In understanding their form, we gain a deeper appreciation for their function as transformative, living words — spoken long ago, and still speaking today.

Chapter 6
Literary, Narrative, and Reader-Response Criticism

Introduction: Reading the Gospels as Stories

For much of modern Gospel scholarship, interpretation focused on sources, forms, and redaction—questions about what lay behind the text. What traditions did the Evangelists or Gospel writers inherit? What sources did they use? How were oral sayings preserved and transmitted? These approaches yielded important insights, but over time, scholars began to ask a new set of questions: What if we focused on the Gospels as they are, not just as they were composed? What if we treated them as literary works—crafted narratives with plot, character, and structure?

These questions gave rise to literary and narrative criticism, approaches that read the Gospels as coherent and intentional stories, not merely as historical documents or containers of tradition. In parallel, reader-response criticism shifted attention from author and source to the role of the reader—exploring how meaning is shaped not only by the text but also by the interpretive communities and contexts in which it is received.

These methods have flourished in recent decades, transforming both academic and devotional engagement with the Gospels. They invite readers into a dynamic interaction with the text, paying attention to how stories are told, what narrative strategies are employed, and how readers are positioned to interpret, question, or even participate in the unfolding drama.

This chapter will introduce the key insights of narrative criticism, literary analysis, and reader-response approaches, showing how these methods offer fresh ways of encountering the Synoptic Gospels. Rather than undermining historical concerns, they complement them, revealing the theological richness and rhetorical artistry of the Evangelists. Through careful attention to plot, characterization, perspective, irony, and reception, we come to see the Gospels not only as records of the past, but as powerful narratives that form faith, identity, and imagination.

Narrative Criticism: Discovering the Story World

Narrative criticism begins with the recognition that the Gospels are stories — not in the sense of fiction, but in the sense of structured, intentional accounts with beginnings, middles, and ends. They contain characters, settings, conflicts, resolutions, and narrative voice. They guide readers through a carefully ordered plot, inviting them to see and feel what the narrator wants them to notice.

This approach emerged in earnest in the late 20th century, with scholars such as R. Alan Culpepper (*Anatomy of the Fourth Gospel*, later adapted for the Synoptics), Robert Tannehill (*The Narrative Unity of Luke-Acts*), and David Rhoads (*Mark as Story*). These scholars emphasized that the Gospels are not random assemblages of tradition but unified literary works that use the tools of narrative to communicate theological truth.

Key concepts in narrative criticism include plot, characterization, narrative time and space, point of view, and reader positioning. The plot refers to the movement of the story — how events are arranged and how tension builds and resolves. In Mark, for example, the plot moves rapidly and urgently toward the cross.

Jesus' identity is shrouded in mystery, his disciples fail to understand, and the ending (Mark 16:8) is famously abrupt. This structure reinforces Mark's central theme: that Jesus is the suffering Son of God, revealed most clearly in his death.

Characterization in the Gospels often works indirectly. Jesus is revealed not through physical description but through actions, dialogue, and the responses of others. The disciples are frequently portrayed with ambiguity — faithful yet flawed, chosen yet confused. Characters like the hemorrhaging woman (Luke 8), Bartimaeus (Mark 10), or the centurion at the cross (Matt 27) often exhibit insight and faith in contrast to the expected religious authorities. These portrayals draw readers into the text, inviting reflection on what it means to see, believe, and follow.

Narrative space and time also carry theological weight. The journey from Galilee to Jerusalem, especially in Luke's long "travel narrative" (Luke 9:51–19:27), is not just geographical; it is symbolic of the path of discipleship and prophetic mission. Time may be compressed or expanded, depending on narrative focus. Events like the Transfiguration, which occupy only a few verses, may carry enormous theological significance, revealing divine identity in a moment of luminous vision.

A particularly important feature of narrative criticism is attention to the implied narrator and the implied reader. The narrator controls what information is given, how characters are introduced, and when irony or ambiguity is allowed to flourish. The implied reader is the audience the text assumes — someone who is expected to understand certain cultural or scriptural references, to sympathize with some characters and question others. For example, when Jesus asks, "Who do you say that I am?" (Mark 8:29), the question is directed to the disciples—but also to the reader, who has been given more insight than the characters within the story. This technique, called dramatic irony, creates space for reflection, confession, and even self-examination.

Narrative criticism thus opens up the Gospels as carefully crafted theological dramas, where meaning is not only found in individual sayings but in the way the story unfolds, how characters develop, and how readers are drawn into the journey of discipleship.

Literary Criticism: Themes, Structure, and Symbolism

Closely related to narrative criticism, literary criticism engages the Gospels with the broader tools of literary analysis. It explores themes, symbolism, metaphor, intertextuality, and rhetorical strategies. This approach sees the Gospels not merely as theological documents but as works of literature, using recognizable techniques to communicate meaning.

One area of focus is repetition and structure. Matthew, for example, arranges his Gospel into five major teaching blocks (chs. 5–7, 10, 13, 18, 23–25), often introduced with a formula such as "When Jesus had finished saying these things..." This structure likely echoes the five books of Moses, presenting Jesus as the new lawgiver, a teacher whose words carry divine authority. Literary critics also note how parables, beatitudes, and woes are grouped and balanced for rhetorical effect.

Mark's Gospel employs intercalation, or "sandwiching," in which one story is inserted into the middle of another. This device invites readers to interpret the two stories in relation to one another. A famous example occurs in Mark 5, where Jesus is on his way to heal Jairus's daughter when he is interrupted by the woman with the flow of blood. The combination of these healing stories deepens the theme of faith, interruption, and restoration, showing how Jesus' power reaches the desperate and marginalized.

Literary criticism also pays attention to symbolism and metaphor. In Luke, light and darkness, poverty and reversal, joy and fulfillment are recurring motifs. Jesus' table fellowship is more than hospitality — it is symbolic of the inclusive kingdom that welcomes sinners and outsiders. The road, the house, the vineyard, and the sea are more than physical spaces — they often function as metaphorical landscapes, framing divine-human encounters.

One of the strengths of literary criticism is that it allows us to read the Gospels as coherent and artful wholes, without fragmenting the text into isolated traditions. It complements historical methods by helping readers see how theology is embedded in the form, flow, and feel of the text itself. The Gospels are not just records of what Jesus did and said — they are carefully told stories about who he is, designed to evoke response, faith, and transformation.

Reader-Response Criticism: The Meaning-Making Role of the Reader

While narrative and literary criticism emphasize how stories are constructed, reader-response criticism shifts the spotlight to the reader's role in constructing meaning. This approach emerged from developments in literary theory during the late twentieth century, particularly in the work of scholars such as Wolfgang Iser, Stanley Fish, and, within biblical studies, Norman Petersen and Edgar McKnight. It asks not just, "What does the text say?" but "How does the reader experience and interpret the text — and how do different contexts shape that experience?"

Reader-response critics argue that texts are not static containers of meaning. Rather, they are dynamic invitations, open to engagement, interpretation, and even contestation. Meaning does not reside solely in the author's intent or the text's formal structure, but emerges through the interaction between text and reader, shaped by the reader's cultural location, questions, and expectations.

This approach is especially fruitful in Gospel studies because the Synoptic Gospels are richly textured narratives designed to evoke a response. Readers are not neutral observers — they are drawn into the story world, invited to identify with characters, to ponder Jesus' questions, to feel the tensions, and to make decisions. The parables, in particular, function as open texts, prompting reflection rather than prescribing doctrine. For instance, the parable of the sower (Mark 4:1-20) doesn't simply inform — it invites readers to examine their own receptivity to the word. The story's meaning unfolds differently depending on who hears it, and from where.

Reader-response criticism also opens space for plurality of interpretation. A first-century Jewish follower of Jesus, a fourth-century North African bishop, a medieval monk, a modern feminist theologian, and a rural lay reader in the global South may each read the same text with different questions and find different kinds of meaning. Rather than treating this as a problem, reader-response theory sees it as a strength. The Gospels are living texts — rooted in history, yet responsive to the Spirit-led reading of diverse communities.

Within this approach, scholars also attend to how the text positions the reader. The Gospels often lead readers to identify with certain characters — sometimes with those who fail or question, like Peter, the disciples, or the crowds. These identifications create space for empathy, humility, and self-examination. At times, the reader is given more knowledge than the characters (dramatic irony), as in Mark's passion narrative. At other times, the reader is left with unanswered questions, as in the enigmatic ending of Mark 16:8. These narrative strategies create a reading experience that is active rather than passive, drawing the audience into the interpretive process.

Reader-response criticism thus reminds us that interpretation is always contextual, relational, and participatory. It resists the notion of a single, fixed meaning and invites readers to engage the text as encounter, as dialogue, and as a space for spiritual, ethical, and theological reflection.

Conclusion: Reading the Gospels as Literary-Theological Testimony

The turn to literary, narrative, and reader-response criticism has marked a profound shift in Gospel studies — a shift from excavation to engagement, from analysis of background to attention to how the text functions in its present form and reception. These methods have not replaced historical-critical tools; rather, they offer a complementary set of lenses through which to understand the Gospels as crafted stories that speak powerfully and persuasively to their readers.

Narrative criticism has helped us see the Gospels as coherent, dramatic, and artfully constructed. We have learned to follow the arc of the story, to attend to character development, and to pay attention to the interplay of setting, timing, and voice. We have come to see how theology is not always declared but often shown — through plot, irony, and interaction.

Literary criticism has drawn our attention to themes, patterns, structures, and symbols — helping us to notice how repetition, metaphor, and rhetorical design function to deepen theological meaning. It reminds us that the Gospel writers were not only theologians and historians, but also artists of the word, using literary tools to evoke insight and transformation.

Reader-response criticism, in turn, has invited us to reflect on how meaning emerges in the act of reading. It challenges us to read not just for what the text meant, but for what it means—to us, here and now, in community, in worship, and in life. It honors the diversity of perspectives within the global church and encourages humility, openness, and attentiveness to the Spirit in the act of interpretation.

Together, these approaches remind us that the Synoptic Gospels are not just about Jesus—they are written to shape us as his followers. They tell stories not only to inform but to form. They challenge, comfort, provoke, and inspire. They speak not only from the past but into the present, inviting us to follow the way of Jesus with our imaginations awakened, our convictions deepened, and our hearts attuned to the story of God's kingdom breaking into the world.

Chapter 7
Postcolonial, Liberationist, and Contextual Approaches

Introduction: Reading from the Margins

For much of Christian history, biblical interpretation was shaped by Western, male, Eurocentric contexts — often disconnected from the struggles of oppressed and marginalized peoples. In the last several decades, however, new currents of Gospel interpretation have emerged, rooted in the lived experiences of suffering, resistance, and hope. These readings — whether labeled postcolonial, liberationist, feminist, womanist, queer, or contextual — insist that the Gospels are not neutral texts, nor are interpreters detached from social location. Rather, the Synoptic Gospels are texts of power, protest, and promise, whose meaning is discovered in dialogue with real-world contexts of injustice and aspiration.

This chapter explores a range of approaches that interpret the Synoptic Gospels from the perspective of those on the underside of history. These readings take seriously the imperial and political world of Jesus, the radical nature of his teachings and actions, and the contemporary relevance of his message for communities facing exploitation, violence, and exclusion. Whether shaped by Latin American liberation theology, African postcolonial critique, Asian feminist thought, or Black and queer hermeneutics, these approaches call the church and academy to read with eyes open to empire, injustice, and the liberating Spirit of God.

The Gospels and Empire: Reading Against the Grain

The Roman Empire looms large behind the Synoptic Gospels. Jesus was born, lived, and was crucified under Roman rule. He was hailed as "Son of God" and "Lord" — titles claimed by Caesar. His message of the "kingdom of God" challenged the reigning vision of power, peace, and order proclaimed by Rome. Yet for centuries, Gospel interpretation often ignored this imperial backdrop, spiritualizing Jesus' message and detaching it from the political realities of his world.

In the past few decades, scholars have increasingly emphasized the anti-imperial dimensions of the Gospels. Richard Horsley, in works such as *Jesus and Empire*, argues that Jesus' proclamation of God's reign was a direct confrontation with imperial power structures. His healings, meals, exorcisms, and parables all functioned as acts of resistance, asserting divine authority over against Roman domination and its local enablers. Warren Carter, in *Matthew and Empire*, shows how Matthew's Gospel subverts imperial language, offering Jesus — not Caesar — as the true Son of God, bringer of peace, and ruler of the nations.

Postcolonial readings continue this work by asking how the Gospels both resist and reflect imperial logic. Scholars like R. S. Sugirtharajah and Tat-siong Benny Liew explore how colonial and neocolonial readings of Scripture have perpetuated oppression, often by aligning Jesus with empire rather than resistance. They challenge interpreters to decolonize their readings, to notice where imperial ideology seeps into the text or its reception, and to reclaim the Gospels as texts of liberation for the colonized and dispossessed.

These approaches do not ignore the theological depth of the Gospels — they deepen it. They remind us that the Gospels tell the story of a crucified man, executed by the state, whose followers proclaimed his resurrection as God's vindication. This is a profoundly political story, one that continues to speak powerfully in contexts of military occupation, police violence, economic exploitation, and resistance movements around the world.

Liberationist Readings: Gospel Hope from Below

Liberation theology emerged in Latin America in the 1960s and 70s, shaped by the experiences of poverty, dictatorship, and economic inequality. Theologians such as Gustavo Gutiérrez (*A Theology of Liberation*), Leonardo Boff, and José Míguez Bonino argued that theology must begin not with abstract dogma but with the lived experience of the poor, and that Scripture should be read from the perspective of those who suffer injustice. From this location, the Gospels become a source of prophetic critique and hope, revealing a God who sides with the oppressed and calls for radical transformation.

In liberationist readings, Jesus appears as liberator and prophet — one who proclaims good news to the poor, sets the oppressed free, and denounces systems of inequality. The Sermon on the Plain in Luke (6:20–26), with its blessings for the poor and woes for the rich, becomes a central text. Parables such as the Rich Man and Lazarus (Luke 16:19–31) or the Workers in the Vineyard (Matt 20.1–16) are read not as moral tales but as revolutionary reimaginings of justice, economy, and dignity.

Liberationist interpretation is not only analytical — it is praxis-oriented. It insists that biblical interpretation must lead to action: organizing, advocacy, and solidarity with the marginalized. The Gospels are read in base communities, in prisons, in slums, and on the streets—not as a source of escapism, but as a call to liberating discipleship.

Liberation theology has spread far beyond Latin America, taking root in Black theology, Dalit theology, minjung theology, and other movements around the globe. In each case, the Synoptic Gospels become a living word in the midst of struggle, a source of resistance, reimagination, and resurrection.

Postcolonial Criticism: Decentering the Dominant

Postcolonial criticism builds on the insights of liberation theology but takes a more literary and cultural approach, analyzing how texts and readers are shaped by the legacies of colonialism and empire. It examines not only how the Gospels resist empire, but also how they have been used—consciously or not—to justify conquest, slavery, and subjugation.

Postcolonial critics ask: Who is speaking in this text? Whose perspective is centered? Who is silenced, erased, or othered? They notice how ethnic, cultural, and geographical markers function to include or exclude. They explore how biblical texts have been weaponized in colonized contexts and how they might now be reclaimed and reinterpreted from the margins.

Kwok Pui-lan, in *Postcolonial Imagination and Feminist Theology*, urges readers to take seriously the voices of Asian women, indigenous communities, and those at the edges of empire. She challenges dominant interpretations of Jesus' identity and mission, seeking a more inclusive and hybrid theology. Musa Dube, writing from Botswana, critiques missionary interpretations that stripped African communities of dignity and culture, and proposes a decolonized reading of the Gospels that lifts up healing, restoration, and indigenous wisdom.

Postcolonial readings are often suspicious of universalizing claims. They insist that all interpretation is contextual, and that the voices of those previously excluded — women, colonized peoples, enslaved communities, diasporic identities — must now be centered in biblical scholarship. They remind us that Jesus himself was a colonized subject, living under occupation, speaking from the periphery, and challenging systems of religious and political domination.

Feminist, Womanist, and Queer Interpretations: Reclaiming the Margins

While postcolonial and liberationist readings focus primarily on the social, political, and economic dimensions of oppression, feminist, womanist, and queer readings of the Synoptic Gospels attend especially to questions of gender, sexuality, power, and voice. These approaches challenge the patriarchal structures that have long shaped biblical interpretation, calling attention to the experiences and insights of women, Black women in particular, and LGBTQ+ persons, both in the text and among its interpreters.

Feminist criticism asks how women are portrayed in the Gospels, how their roles are narrated, and how traditional readings have often ignored or diminished their agency. Scholars like Elisabeth Schüssler Fiorenza, in *In Memory of Her*, argue that early Christian communities included active female disciples and leaders, and that the memory of these women has been suppressed or distorted in later theological tradition. The Synoptic Gospels, while written within patriarchal cultures, contain numerous narratives in which women demonstrate profound faith, insight, and courage — whether in the hemorrhaging woman who reaches out for healing (Mark 5), the Syrophoenician woman who challenges Jesus (Mark 7), or the women who remain near the cross and become the first witnesses to the resurrection (Mark 15–16; Matt 28; Luke 24).

Womanist theology, emerging from the lived experience of African American women, deepens this critique by attending to the intersections of race, class, and gender. Womanist scholars such as Renita Weems, Delores Williams, and Clarice Martin explore how Black women have often been erased from theological discourse, and how Gospel stories can be reclaimed as resources of resilience, survival, and sacred worth. For example, the persistence of the woman with the alabaster jar (Luke 7:36–50) or the lament of the women of Jerusalem (Luke 23:27–31) become entry points for reading Scripture as solidarity with the suffering and dignity in resistance.

Queer biblical criticism takes a different angle, interrogating how assumptions about gender and sexuality have shaped interpretation and how biblical texts might be read in ways that affirm queer lives and identities. Scholars like Tat-siong Benny Liew, Ken Stone, and Teresa Hornsby challenge heteronormative readings of Scripture, explore the fluidity of gender roles and bodies in the Gospels, and ask how Jesus' interactions with marginalized individuals model radical inclusion. Some interpretations focus on the ambiguity of certain relationships, the hospitality extended to eunuchs and outsiders, or the queering of power in Jesus' rejection of dominance and his embrace of vulnerability.

Together, feminist, womanist, and queer readings of the Synoptic Gospels offer not only critique, but also reconstruction. They insist that interpretation is never neutral, that silence and erasure must be named, and that the Gospel of Jesus Christ speaks most powerfully when it elevates the voices of the marginalized, affirms the sacredness of all bodies and identities, and challenges the structures — both ancient and modern — that perpetuate exclusion and harm.

Contextual Approaches from the Global Church

Interpretation of the Synoptic Gospels has also been invigorated by voices from across the Global South, where communities read Scripture not only through academic lenses but through the urgency of lived realities. In Africa, biblical interpretation is often shaped by communal values, oral storytelling, and ancestral memory. Scholars such as Madipoane Masenya and Musa Dube bring to the fore readings that engage with HIV/AIDS, economic injustice, gender violence, and postcolonial trauma. In these readings, Jesus appears as a healer and restorer, and the Gospel as a source of hope and solidarity in the face of suffering.

In Asia, interpreters highlight themes of diaspora, hybridity, family, and resistance to colonial and patriarchal structures. Figures like Kwok Pui-lan, Gale Yee, and Jung Young Lee explore how Gospel texts intersect with Confucian ethics, communal identity, and the realities of immigrant and Asian American experience. Jesus' concern for the stranger, the outcast, and the vulnerable resonates deeply in cultures marked by fragmentation, migration, and cultural negotiation.

In Latin America, the Gospel has long been read through the lens of poverty, indigenous struggle, and land rights. The stories of Jesus — particularly his healings, exorcisms, and parables of reversal — are interpreted as signs of liberation, calling communities to resist oppression and work for justice. Indigenous Christian interpretations often read the Gospels in light of land-based spirituality, collective identity, and decolonized worldviews, affirming the Gospel as a call to restoration and communal flourishing.

These global contextual readings do not merely supplement traditional interpretation — they decenter the Western gaze, challenging theological monocultures and insisting on the plurality and resilience of Gospel meaning across languages, cultures, and histories. They remind us that the Jesus of the Gospels speaks many languages, walks many roads, and continues to reveal himself wherever people hunger for justice, healing, and hope.

Conclusion: Interpretation as Liberation and Responsibility

Postcolonial, liberationist, and contextual readings of the Synoptic Gospels represent not a departure from faithful interpretation, but a return to the radical edge of the Gospel tradition. They recover the voices of the wounded, the silenced, the excluded — the very people Jesus consistently centered in his ministry. They remind us that Jesus did not speak from the halls of power, but from the hillsides, the marketplaces, the margins. He broke bread with sinners, called out corrupt leaders, healed the broken, and spoke in parables that disrupted complacency and revealed the heart of God.

These approaches challenge modern interpreters to read with ethical awareness, to examine our own positions of privilege or precarity, and to ask: Whose voices are missing in our interpretations? Whose experiences are ignored? What assumptions do we bring to the text — and whom do they serve?

To read the Gospels today is not only an academic task — it is a moral and communal act. The Synoptic Gospels are not only about what God did then; they invite us to discern what God is doing now. They proclaim a kingdom where the poor are blessed, the hungry are filled, and the last are made first. They speak of a crucified Lord whose resurrection is not a private consolation but a cosmic declaration that life will rise where empire has tried to kill.

Reading with liberation in mind does not mean that every interpretation must be political in a partisan sense. It means that every reading is accountable — to the community, to the suffering, to the hope of justice, and to the Gospel itself. It is a call to interpretation as solidarity, as resistance, and as resurrection faith.

Chapter 8
Comparing the Synoptic Gospels

Introduction: Seeing Together, Listening Distinctly

The term "Synoptic" means "seen together." Matthew, Mark, and Luke are called the Synoptic Gospels because they present a remarkably similar account of Jesus' life, ministry, death, and resurrection. Their shared structure, overlapping stories, and often near-identical wording allow them to be read side-by-side in a Gospel synopsis. Yet careful readers quickly notice that these Gospels, while closely related, are also strikingly distinct—in vocabulary, narrative shape, theological emphasis, and portrayal of Jesus and his followers.

This chapter invites readers to explore both the common ground and the unique theological profiles of each Gospel. It offers a comparative study that highlights major areas of overlap (such as the triple tradition), distinctive themes (such as the kingdom of God, discipleship, and Christology), and characteristic features of each Evangelist's presentation of Jesus. Through this comparison, we come to appreciate how the Synoptic Gospels are not repetitive accounts, but complementary testimonies—three voices, each shaped by particular communities and convictions, bearing witness to the same Jesus in different yet resonant ways.

Shared Material and Narrative Patterns

The Synoptic Gospels exhibit remarkable similarity in their broad narrative structure. All three begin (in effect) with the baptism of Jesus, describe his

Galilean ministry, depict a journey to Jerusalem, and culminate in the passion, crucifixion, and resurrection. These core events form the skeleton of the Synoptic tradition, and their consistency suggests that the Evangelists drew upon shared traditions—oral and written—and sought to present Jesus' story in a broadly recognizable sequence.

This shared material is most clearly evident in what scholars call the "triple tradition"—passages that appear in all three Gospels. Examples include Jesus' baptism (Mark 1:9–11 // Matt 3:13–17 // Luke 3:21–22), the feeding of the five thousand (Mark 6:30–44 // Matt 14:13–21 // Luke 9:10–17), the transfiguration, and most of the passion narrative. These stories are often recounted with similar phrasing in Greek, suggesting literary dependence, as described in Chapter 2.

Matthew and Luke also share material not found in Mark—such as the Beatitudes, the Lord's Prayer, and parables like the lost sheep and the wise and foolish builders. This "double tradition" is a key feature of the Two-Source Hypothesis and may derive from the hypothesized Q source. Even in these shared passages, however, Matthew and Luke differ significantly in order, framing, and wording, revealing their editorial and theological priorities.

In contrast, each Gospel also contains unique material. Matthew includes the visit of the magi, the Sermon on the Mount, and a developed teaching on the church (Matt 16:18–19; 18:15–20). Luke offers the parables of the Good Samaritan and the Prodigal Son, an extended birth narrative with Mary's Magnificat and Zechariah's Benedictus, and a focus on prayer, the Holy Spirit, and inclusion. Mark, though the shortest, includes vivid narrative detail, an aura of urgency, and a tone of mystery and ambiguity that is distinctive.

These patterns suggest not only a shared tradition but also creative theological interpretation. The Evangelists or Gospel writers did not merely record what was passed on to them; they reshaped it in light of the concerns, hopes, and identities of their communities. Comparison allows us to honor the unity and diversity of their witness.

Theological Themes in Comparison

While the Synoptic Gospels share a common story, they emphasize different aspects of that story. These differences are not contradictions; they are theological accents, each illuminating the person and mission of Jesus from a unique angle.

A central theme in all three Gospels is the kingdom of God. Mark introduces Jesus' public ministry with a declaration of kingdom urgency: "The time is fulfilled, and the kingdom of God has come near" (Mark 1:15). Matthew expands this theme, using the phrase "kingdom of heaven" (a Jewish reverential circumlocution) and presenting Jesus' teaching—especially in the Sermon on the Mount—as the ethical foundation of kingdom living. Luke portrays the kingdom with an emphasis on reversal and inclusion, announcing good news to the poor, release to the captives, and the lifting up of the lowly (Luke 4:18–19; 6:20–26). Across the Synoptics, the kingdom is both present and future, personal and social, ethical and apocalyptic.

Discipleship is another key theme. All three Gospels present Jesus calling disciples to leave behind family, occupation, and security to follow him. But they develop this theme in distinctive ways. Mark emphasizes the cost and difficulty of discipleship, portraying the disciples as slow to understand and often missing the point. In Matthew, the disciples are more capable, and Jesus is portrayed as a teacher, forming them through structured instruction. Luke presents discipleship as a journey of transformation, often highlighting hospitality, prayer, and the guidance of the Holy Spirit.

Each Gospel also develops a distinctive Christology. Mark portrays Jesus as the suffering Son of Man, whose identity is veiled and revealed primarily through the cross. Matthew emphasizes Jesus as the fulfillment of Scripture, the new Moses, and the one who brings the story of Israel to completion. Luke highlights Jesus as a Spirit-anointed prophet, a friend of the marginalized, and the inaugurator of a new age of salvation. These theological portraits are not mutually exclusive, but they reflect different emphases, each shaped by Scripture, tradition, and pastoral context.

Literary Features, Vocabulary, and Emphasis

In addition to thematic differences, the Synoptic Gospels exhibit distinctive literary styles and vocabularies that reflect the theological aims of each Evangelist. These variations help readers not only appreciate each Gospel on its own terms but also notice how storytelling and theological purpose go hand in hand.

Mark's style is famously vivid and fast-paced. He favors simple sentence constructions, frequent use of the Greek word *euthus* ("immediately"), and a narrative that moves with breathless urgency. His Gospel is full of action, often shifting quickly from one event to another. Mark includes numerous minor characters, emotional reactions, and dramatic irony. The disciples repeatedly misunderstand Jesus, and the story concludes not with triumph but with ambiguity and fear (Mark 16:8). These features reflect Mark's theological emphasis on the mystery and cost of discipleship, the suffering Messiah, and the challenge of following Jesus in the face of misunderstanding and fear.

Matthew's Gospel is more formal, structured, and didactic. It is the most overtly Jewish of the Synoptics, filled with scriptural quotations, fulfillment formulas, and references to Jewish law and custom. Matthew prefers the phrase "kingdom of heaven," likely out of reverence for the divine name, and arranges much of Jesus' teaching into organized discourses, including the Sermon on the Mount (chs. 5–7), the missionary discourse (ch. 10), and the parables of the kingdom (ch. 13). The vocabulary is often more elevated and polished than Mark's, and the tone is that of a rabbi or scribe training a new community. Matthew's Jesus is a teacher and interpreter of Torah, one who calls for a righteousness that goes beyond surface observance to the deeper demands of love and justice.

Luke's Gospel is marked by elegance, breadth, and inclusivity. The Greek is more sophisticated than in Mark or Matthew, and Luke writes with the style of a Hellenistic historian (as his introduction in Luke 1:1–4 suggests). He frequently uses parallel stories, poetic songs (such as the Magnificat and Benedictus), and long narrative sections, including the travel narrative (Luke 9:51–19:27), which presents Jesus' journey to Jerusalem as a theological pilgrimage. Luke also places strong emphasis on the Holy Spirit, the role of women, prayer, and reversal—lifting up the lowly and casting down the proud. His Jesus is a compassionate and prophetic figure, one who brings salvation to outsiders and proclaims a gospel of joy and justice.

Each Gospel writer thus brings a unique literary voice and theological vision to the shared story of Jesus. Their different choices in structure, tone, vocabulary, and narrative development invite readers to listen attentively and to see the same story from multiple angles — much as a diamond reveals different facets depending on how it is held to the light.

Comparative Case Studies

To understand how these Gospel distinctions function in practice, we can examine a few key parallel stories, observing how each Evangelist adapts and interprets shared tradition. These case studies highlight not only textual variations but also deeper theological commitments.

The Baptism of Jesus

In Mark 1:9–11, the baptism is described with economy and drama. Jesus comes from Galilee, is baptized by John, and immediately sees the heavens torn open and the Spirit descending like a dove. A voice speaks directly to Jesus: "You are my Son, the Beloved." Mark emphasizes Jesus' divine identity and the rupture between heaven and earth, suggesting the apocalyptic nature of his mission.

Matthew's account (3:13–17) expands the scene by including a dialogue between Jesus and John. John protests, saying that he should be baptized by Jesus. Jesus responds, "Let it be so now; for it is proper for us in this way to fulfill all righteousness." This exchange deflects possible concerns about why the sinless Jesus is baptized and emphasizes his role as the obedient servant who fulfills God's will and the Scriptures.

Luke's version (3:21–22) is even more concise, omitting John's involvement altogether and placing the emphasis on Jesus' prayer and the descent of the Spirit. The voice from heaven speaks similarly but serves as part of Luke's wider motif of divine affirmation and Spirit empowerment. The scene introduces themes of prophetic mission, prayerful dependence, and divine guidance, which recur throughout Luke–Acts.

The Transfiguration

All three Synoptics narrate the Transfiguration (Mark 9:2–8; Matt 17:1–8; Luke 9:28–36), in which Jesus is revealed in glory, accompanied by Moses and Elijah, and affirmed by a voice from heaven. In Mark, the focus is on the disciples' fear, the mystery of the event, and Jesus' command to remain silent until after the resurrection. This continues Mark's theme of the "Messianic Secret" — Jesus must not be misunderstood as merely a wonder-worker or triumphant leader.

Matthew adds important interpretive elements. He includes a detail that the disciples fall on their faces in fear and are reassured by Jesus. The voice says not only "This is my Son" but adds, "listen to him," echoing Deuteronomy 18:15 and reinforcing Jesus as the promised prophet like Moses. The emphasis is on divine revelation and Jesus' authority as interpreter of God's will.

Luke's account emphasizes Jesus' conversation with Moses and Elijah about his "departure" (exodus) that he was about to accomplish at Jerusalem — a clear link between this moment of glory and the suffering to come. Luke also notes that the disciples were sleepy, echoing Gethsemane, and that Peter speaks without understanding. The emphasis is not only on Jesus' identity but also on the continuity between his suffering and his mission, a major Lukan theme.

The Passion Narrative

The Synoptic passion narratives all portray Jesus' arrest, trial, crucifixion, and death, but their tone and theological framing differ.

Mark presents the passion with raw intensity. Jesus is abandoned by his disciples, mocked by onlookers, and cries out from the cross in anguish, "My God, my God, why have you forsaken me?" (Mark 15:34). There is no resurrection appearance, and the women flee in fear. Mark's Jesus suffers deeply, embodying the scandal and cost of the cross.

Matthew retains much of Mark's structure but adds powerful apocalyptic signs: the temple veil is torn, an earthquake occurs, and tombs are opened (Matt 27:51-53). These details highlight the cosmic significance of Jesus' death and its fulfillment of prophecy. The centurion exclaims, "Truly this was God's Son!" (27:54), echoing Matthew's theme of recognition and fulfillment.

Luke's passion narrative is more composed and imbued with grace. Jesus is portrayed as in control, forgiving his executioners ("Father, forgive them"), comforting the repentant thief ("Today you will be with me in paradise"), and commending his spirit to God with peace ("Father, into your hands I commend my spirit"). Luke emphasizes divine compassion, innocent suffering, and the extension of salvation even in the final hour.

These comparative examples demonstrate how the Synoptic Gospels, while sharing the same basic story, offer distinct theological portraits of Jesus, each shaped by particular concerns and contexts. The Evangelists are not contradicting one another — they are interpreting together, helping us see the depth and fullness of the Gospel.

Why Comparative Study Matters

Comparing the Synoptic Gospels is not merely an academic exercise — it is a practice of theological discernment, literary appreciation, and spiritual attentiveness. By placing Matthew, Mark, and Luke side by side, we begin to see not only what they share, but also what they emphasize, what they reinterpret, and how they form communities through distinct theological voices.

This comparative approach honors the diversity within unity that characterizes the New Testament. The early church did not preserve a single Gospel. Instead, it canonized four, acknowledging that no one account could exhaust the meaning of Jesus' life and message. The differences among the Synoptics are not problems to be solved or smoothed away—they are gifts to be received, offering complementary insights into the mystery of Christ.

When we compare the Gospels, we develop a greater awareness of how theology works in narrative form. We see that Matthew's Jesus is a teacher who fulfills Torah, that Mark's Jesus is a suffering Son of God who calls disciples into costly following, and that Luke's Jesus is a prophet of compassion and reversal. Each Gospel, in its own way, proclaims the kingdom of God and invites a response of faith—but the shape of that invitation varies, offering space for diverse expressions of discipleship.

Comparative study also deepens our understanding of how the Evangelists shaped their materials. As we saw in Chapter 4, each writer reworked earlier traditions—especially Mark—to address the questions and needs of their own communities. Through redaction, arrangement, and storytelling choices, they communicated not just facts about Jesus, but interpretive frameworks that shaped identity, worship, and mission. By comparing their accounts, we learn how theology is expressed not only in what is said, but in how stories are told.

Finally, comparative reading cultivates a posture of humility. It reminds us that no single voice or community holds a monopoly on truth. In an age that often prizes certainty and uniformity, the Synoptic Gospels teach us to live with complexity, to appreciate nuance, and to listen across difference. They model a form of theological conversation in which unity is not sameness, and in which truth is revealed through dialogue and multiplicity.

Applications for Teaching, Preaching, and Formation

For those who teach, preach, or lead in faith communities, comparative study of the Synoptic Gospels offers practical tools for deeper engagement and formation. It encourages interpreters to slow down, to ask better questions, and to guide others in appreciating the distinctive voices of Scripture.

In the sanctuary, devotional or study setting, and classroom, using a Gospel synopsis or parallel texts enables readers to discover patterns for themselves. They learn to notice variations in phrasing, structure, and theological emphasis—and to wrestle with what those differences mean. Comparative reading sharpens critical thinking and helps careful readers move beyond surface readings or harmonization.

In preaching, the distinct emphases of each Gospel can shape the tone and focus of proclamation. A sermon from Matthew might explore Jesus as teacher and fulfillment; a sermon from Mark might highlight urgency, ambiguity, and discipleship under pressure; a sermon from Luke might emphasize divine mercy, joy, and hospitality. Recognizing these differences helps preachers avoid generic messages and instead proclaim the text with authenticity and clarity.

In spiritual formation, reading the Synoptics comparatively cultivates attentiveness. It helps individuals and communities discover how different aspects of Jesus' identity and mission speak to different seasons of life. For the suffering, Mark's Jesus may offer solidarity and strength. For the uncertain, Luke's Jesus may offer joy and reassurance. For those seeking wisdom, Matthew's Jesus may provide guidance and grounding. These voices work together—not in competition but in chorus—to shape whole-person discipleship.

Conclusion: A Symphony of Witness

Matthew, Mark, and Luke stand together as a symphony of theological witness—three distinct but harmonious voices that proclaim the good news of God's reign through the story of Jesus Christ. Their similarities draw us into the shared memory of the early church. Their differences invite us to explore the richness and breadth of Gospel meaning.

To compare the Synoptic Gospels is to become a better listener—more attentive to differences in language, more responsive to nuance, more open to the Spirit speaking through multiplicity. It is to enter a dialogue across time and community, in which the face of Christ appears in many dimensions: teacher, prophet, healer, liberator, crucified Messiah, risen Lord.

In a world of division, the Synoptic Gospels offer not only truth, but a model of theological diversity held together by shared confession. They remind us that the Gospel is not one-dimensional. It is a living word, told and retold, remembered and reimagined, spoken anew in every context. As we listen to these three different Evangelists, we are invited to find our place in their story—and to bear witness in our own voices to the God who still speaks.

Chapter 9
The Synoptic Gospels and the Hebrew Scriptures

Introduction: One Story, Many Echoes

From the first verses of the New Testament, it is clear that the Evangelists or Gospel writers do not understand the story of Jesus as something entirely new. Rather, they present it as the climax of a much older story — the story of Israel, of God's promises, of the covenant people, the law, the prophets, and the hope for redemption. For the writers of Matthew, Mark, and Luke, the life, death, and resurrection of Jesus only make full sense when read in light of the Scriptures of Israel, known to Christians as the Old Testament.

Throughout the Synoptic Gospels, the Hebrew Scriptures are quoted, alluded to, and echoed in ways both subtle and explicit. These scriptural connections are not mere ornament; they are central to the Evangelists' theological claims. They shape how the audience is meant to understand Jesus — his genealogy, birth, mission, teachings, suffering, and resurrection. They also frame his story as one of fulfillment and continuity, even as he offers new interpretations and radical calls.

This chapter explores the many ways the Synoptic Gospels engage the Hebrew Bible — through explicit citations, implicit echoes, typological patterns, and theological re-readings. By studying these connections, we gain deeper insight into how early Christian communities understood Jesus as both rooted in Jewish tradition and transforming it from within.

Quotations and Fulfillment in Matthew

Among the Synoptic Evangelists, Matthew is the most explicit in his use of the Hebrew Scriptures. From the opening genealogy (Matt 1:1–17), which traces Jesus' lineage through David and Abraham, Matthew presents Jesus as the culmination of Israel's story. His frequent use of the formula "This was to fulfill what was spoken by the prophet…" signals his intent: to show that the events of Jesus' life were anticipated in Scripture.

Matthew's Gospel includes at least a dozen fulfillment citations, each linking a specific event in Jesus' life to a prophetic text. When Jesus is born of a virgin, Matthew cites Isaiah 7:14 ("a virgin shall conceive and bear a son") as fulfilled in that event (Matt 1:22–23). When Herod massacres the infants, Matthew draws on Jeremiah 31:15 ("Rachel weeping for her children") to frame this horror within the sorrow of exile (Matt 2:17–18). When Jesus begins his ministry in Galilee, Matthew sees this as fulfilling Isaiah's prophecy of a great light shining in the land of Zebulun and Naphtali (Matt 4:14–16; Isa 9:1–2).

These citations serve both apologetic and theological functions. They assure Matthew's Jewish-Christian readers that belief in Jesus does not require abandoning the Scriptures—instead, it reveals their deeper meaning. At the same time, these fulfillment texts show that the story of Jesus is not an accident of history but part of God's long-promised plan for Israel and the world.

Matthew also engages in typology, presenting Jesus as a new Moses and a new Israel. The flight to Egypt and return (Matt 2:13–15) echoes the Exodus. The temptation in the wilderness mirrors Israel's testing (Matt 4:1–11; Deut 6–8). The Sermon on the Mount evokes Sinai, with Jesus ascending the mountain to deliver divine teaching. In these ways, Matthew shows

Jesus not only fulfilling prophecy but reenacting and redeeming Israel's story.

Scriptural Framework and Implicit Allusions in Mark

Mark, while less explicit in his use of Scripture than Matthew, nevertheless weaves the Hebrew Bible into his narrative in profound and sophisticated ways. Mark opens his Gospel not with a birth narrative but with a scriptural collage: "As it is written in the prophet Isaiah" (Mark 1:2-3). The quotation is actually a composite of Malachi 3:1 and Isaiah 40:3, signaling the prophetic preparation for God's coming and setting the tone for the Gospel as a fulfillment of divine promise.

Throughout Mark, Old Testament allusions appear in the background of Jesus' actions and words. When Jesus teaches in parables, he echoes Isaiah 6, where the prophet is told to speak in ways that harden hearts (Mark 4:10-12). When Jesus enters Jerusalem on a colt, Mark invokes Zechariah 9:9, where a humble king comes to bring peace. When Jesus is crucified and cries out, "My God, my God, why have you forsaken me?" (Mark 15:34), he quotes Psalm 22:1, linking his suffering to the lament of the righteous sufferer.

Mark's allusions are often subtle and symbolic, requiring close attention. The tearing of the temple veil at Jesus' death (Mark 15:38) may suggest a new access to God's presence, an apocalyptic unveiling, or the fulfillment of prophecies of judgment and renewal. The use of "Son of Man" language throughout the Gospel draws on Daniel 7, where a heavenly figure receives authority and vindication after suffering.

While Mark includes fewer direct citations, his Gospel is saturated with scriptural imagery, shaping a theology in which Jesus' life and death recapitulate and reinterpret Israel's sacred story. For Mark, Jesus is the hidden Messiah, the suffering righteous one, and the eschatological Son of Man, all rooted in the hopes and texts of Israel's Scriptures.

Luke's Liturgical and Theological Use of Scripture

Among the Synoptic Evangelists, Luke integrates Scripture not only through quotation and allusion but also through a deeply liturgical and theological lens. His Gospel is saturated with the language, structure, and themes of the Hebrew Scriptures as articulated in the Greek Septuagint, often articulated through songs, prayers, and speeches that resemble the Psalms and prophetic writings.

Luke's infancy narratives (Luke 1–2) are a prime example. The characters of Zechariah, Mary, Simeon, and Anna speak and act like figures from Israel's past. Their songs of praise—the Benedictus, Magnificat, Gloria, and Nunc Dimittis—are filled with quotations, echoes, and theological motifs from the Psalms, Isaiah, and other prophetic books. These texts situate the birth of Jesus within a continuum of divine promise, portraying him as the fulfillment of God's covenant with Israel, especially God's mercy toward the poor and God's faithfulness to Abraham.

Luke 4:16–30 offers another striking example. Here, Jesus reads Isaiah 61 in the synagogue at Nazareth and declares, "Today this scripture has been fulfilled in your hearing." The passage he reads describes good news to the poor, liberty to the captives, and the year of the Lord's favor—a proclamation that becomes Jesus' own mission statement in Luke. Yet the people's violent reaction also anticipates the pattern of prophetic rejection, a theme that recurs throughout the Gospel and Acts.

Luke is also deeply attuned to the theology of promise and fulfillment. The language of "must" (Greek: *dei*, "it is necessary") recurs throughout the

Gospel, especially in reference to Jesus' suffering, death, and resurrection. After the resurrection, Jesus interprets his story to the disciples on the road to Emmaus: "Beginning with Moses and all the prophets, he interpreted to them the things about himself in all the scriptures" (Luke 24:27). Later, he tells them, "Everything written about me in the law of Moses, the prophets, and the psalms must be fulfilled" (24:44).

Luke's presentation of Jesus is not only rooted in Scripture but also reorients how Scripture is to be read. Jesus is portrayed as the key that unlocks the full meaning of Israel's story. In him, the prophetic hopes of deliverance, inclusion, reversal, and redemption find their fulfillment—not by abolishing the old but by drawing it to completion in a new age of salvation history.

Typology and Theological Patterning in the Synoptic Gospels

Beyond direct quotation and overt citation, the Synoptic Gospels often engage in typological interpretation—a theological approach that sees patterns, events, or figures in Israel's Scriptures as foreshadowing and prefiguring realities fulfilled in the life of Jesus.

Typology differs from prediction. It is not a claim that the Old Testament consciously "predicts" Jesus in a narrow sense, but that the story of Jesus echoes and reenacts the larger story of God's work in history. The past becomes a pattern, which the present fills with new significance.

Matthew's Gospel is especially rich in typology. Jesus is presented as a new Moses: he escapes a tyrannical ruler as an infant, spends time in Egypt, passes through water in baptism, ascends a mountain to deliver teaching, and establishes a covenantal community. His genealogy (Matt 1) places him as the culmination of Israel's history. His five major discourses mirror the five books of the Torah. Matthew also uses Israel's exile and return as a typological frame for Jesus' life: "Out of Egypt I have called my son" (Matt 2:15; cf. Hos 11:1) refers both to Israel and to Jesus.

Mark, while less programmatic, also includes typological elements. Jesus is portrayed as the righteous sufferer, echoing the Psalms and the Servant Songs of Isaiah. His journey mirrors that of the prophets: rejected in his hometown, misunderstood by his own, abandoned in the face of death. The tearing of the temple veil at his death may be read typologically as the end of the old order and the inauguration of new access to God's presence (Mark 15:38).

Luke uses typology to trace a salvation-historical arc from creation to the cross and resurrection, and then on to the early church in Acts. Jesus is the culmination of Israel's prophetic tradition, but also the beginning of a universal mission, reaching Gentiles and the ends of the earth. Luke's frequent references to Elijah and Elisha, his use of Isaiah, and his emphasis on Scripture-fulfillment link Jesus' life and work to a long narrative of divine activity, now extended through the Spirit-empowered church.

Typology thus deepens the theological meaning of the Synoptic Gospels. It portrays Jesus not as a divine interruption, but as the climax of a story long in motion, in which God remains faithful, consistent, and creative—bringing new life through familiar patterns.

Conclusion: The Gospels as Fulfillment and Transformation

The Synoptic Gospels are deeply and intentionally intertextual texts. They cannot be read apart from the Scriptures of Israel—not simply as background material, but as essential to their meaning, message, and mission. The Hebrew Bible does not merely prepare for the Gospels; it is their language, worldview, and theological soil.

To read the Synoptic Gospels attentively is to hear the voice of Moses, the prophets, and the psalmists resonating through Jesus' words and deeds. The kingdom he announces is the fulfillment of Israel's longing. The identity he claims is rooted in the promises of David, the suffering of the Servant, and the wisdom of the sages. The community he forms is built not in place of Israel, but from within its hopes — expanded and transformed to include all nations.

Yet this fulfillment is not repetition. Jesus reinterprets the law, offers radical parables, calls for deeper righteousness, and embraces outcasts and enemies. He embodies a reading of Scripture that is at once faithful and surprising — one that honors the past but refuses to be confined by it. His resurrection becomes the ultimate act of re-reading, opening the Scriptures in new ways to reveal that suffering leads to glory, and death to life.

For contemporary readers, this rich interplay between the Gospels and the Hebrew Scriptures invites us into a continuous dialogue with the whole of Scripture. It challenges us to hold the Old and New Testaments not as separate books but as interwoven testimonies to the character, purposes, and faithfulness of God. And it calls us to read all of Scripture in light of Jesus — the one in whom God's promises are yes and amen.

Chapter 10
Women, Gender, and Power in the Synoptic Gospels

Introduction: Seeing Women, Naming Power

The Synoptic Gospels tell stories of healing, liberation, and the inbreaking of God's kingdom. They are narratives in which boundaries are crossed, hierarchies are challenged, and the last are made first. Within these narratives, women appear more frequently and more meaningfully than traditional assumptions have often allowed. They are present as recipients of healing, as prophetic voices, as bold questioners, as faithful disciples, and as witnesses to the crucifixion and resurrection. Yet they are also unnamed, overlooked, and often spoken of rather than spoken with.

This chapter explores the portrayal of women and the dynamics of gender and power in the Synoptic Gospels. It asks how women function in the narrative, how Jesus interacts with them, and what the Gospels suggest about social status, inclusion, and the community of discipleship. Drawing on both close reading and insights from feminist and womanist interpreters, this chapter will show how the Gospels both reflect the patriarchal realities of the first century and offer resources for liberation, affirmation, and theological reimagination.

In attending to these stories, we do more than recover forgotten figures—we gain insight into the radical logic of the kingdom of God, where the overlooked are lifted up and the powerful are brought low. These stories invite contemporary readers to ask not only how women were seen in Jesus' time, but how they are seen — and see themselves — in the church and world today.

Women in the Narrative World of the Gospels

The Synoptic Gospels introduce us to a range of female characters, some named and many unnamed, who appear in crucial moments of Jesus' life and ministry. While men dominate the public spaces of the story — Pharisees, disciples, rulers, and crowds — women often enter the scene as interruptions, whose presence redirects the narrative, exposes deeper truths, or reveals the nature of discipleship more clearly than the actions of the Twelve.

Some women are named — Mary, the mother of Jesus, plays a central role in Matthew and Luke's birth narratives. In Luke, Mary responds to the angel Gabriel with faithful obedience and speaks the Magnificat, a radical song of reversal and liberation (Luke 1:46–55). Mary Magdalene, along with other women from Galilee, is named as a disciple, a witness to the crucifixion, and a key figure in the resurrection narratives (Mark 15:40–41; Matt 28:1–10; Luke 24:1–11). Her presence in all four Gospels at these climactic moments underscores her apostolic significance, even though her later portrayal in church tradition often reduced her to a caricature of sexual sin.

More often, women are unnamed, yet narratively and theologically significant. The bleeding woman in Mark 5:25–34 (also in Matthew and Luke) reaches out to touch Jesus' cloak in hope and desperation. She is not only healed physically but affirmed publicly: "Daughter, your faith has made you well." Her story is a powerful testament to persistence, faith, and reclaiming dignity, especially in the face of ritual impurity and social exclusion.

In Luke 7:36–50, a "sinful woman" anoints Jesus' feet with tears and perfume, while a Pharisee questions her presence and worth. Jesus defends her, interprets her actions as love and faith, and sees her in light of forgiveness rather than the standards used by the Pharisee and others. Thus, this story challenges social boundaries and redefines righteousness, not by legal status or gender, but by humility, hospitality, and love.

Even in parables, women are present. Jesus compares the kingdom of God to a woman kneading leaven into dough (Matt 13:33; Luke 13:20–21), a woman searching for a lost coin (Luke 15:8–10), or a persistent widow who demands justice from a reluctant judge (Luke 18:1–8). These stories elevate domestic experience and feminine agency as theological analogies, affirming that divine truth is revealed in the lives and actions of women as much as men.

Jesus' Interactions with Women: Disruption and Restoration

Jesus' interactions with women in the Synoptic Gospels are consistently marked by respect, attentiveness, and boundary-crossing compassion. In a culture where gender segregation was common and female voices were often dismissed, Jesus speaks directly to women, touches them, receives their touch, listens to their concerns, and praises their faith.

He responds with healing to the bent-over woman in Luke 13, calling her a "daughter of Abraham" — a title of dignity and covenant inclusion. He speaks of the widow of Zarephath (Luke 4:26) as a recipient of divine favor and notices the widow's offering at the temple (Mark 12:41–44; Luke 21:1–4), elevating her meager gift as an act of true generosity. These stories contrast starkly with the behavior of the religious elite, who are often portrayed as proud, greedy, or indifferent.

Perhaps most striking is Jesus' conversation with the Syrophoenician woman in Mark 7:24–30 (paralleled in Matt 15:21–28). Initially, Jesus refuses her request for healing, citing his mission to the children of Israel. She responds with boldness and wit, claiming even the crumbs from the table. Jesus honors her faith and grants her request. This scene has troubled many interpreters, but feminist scholars like Mitzi Smith and Ched Myers see it as a moment of dialogic transformation — a space where Jesus is challenged and the boundaries of his mission are widened through a woman's voice.

In these interactions, Jesus does not simply include women — he allows them to redefine the terms of the conversation, to act as theologians, disciples, and truth-tellers. His consistent affirmation of their presence challenges both ancient and modern assumptions about who speaks, who leads, and who belongs.

Gender, Social Power, and Intersectional Realities

To fully appreciate how the Synoptic Gospels engage gender, we must understand the social structures of the ancient world, especially how gender intersected with status, purity, and power. In first-century Palestinian society, as in much of the Greco-Roman world, patriarchy was normative. Men held authority in households, religious leadership, public life, and legal matters. Women's roles were largely confined to the domestic sphere, and their honor was mostly tied to chastity, obedience, and silence in public.

Yet within this restrictive system, women were not uniform. Social roles were shaped by class, ethnicity, marital status, age, and even ritual condition. A wealthy widow in Jerusalem had far more social capital than a young unmarried Galilean peasant. A woman with a flow of blood, like the one healed by Jesus, was not just suffering physically—she was ritually impure, economically vulnerable, and likely isolated.

This is where intersectionality becomes vital. A term coined by Kimberlé Crenshaw and developed in womanist theology, intersectionality refers to how multiple axes of identity and oppression—such as race, gender, and class—interact to shape experience. In the Synoptic Gospels, we see intersectional realities at work: women who are doubly marginalized, both by gender and by social condition. The hemorrhaging woman, the Syrophoenician mother, and the widow with only two coins are not only "women" in a patriarchal society—they are poor, sick, foreign, or excluded in additional ways.

By foregrounding these intersecting realities, readers today can better understand the radical nature of Jesus' ministry. He does not merely affirm women as a general category; he responds to the concrete needs of specific women, shaped by multiple layers of vulnerability. He treats them with dignity, calls attention to their faith and courage, and centers them in the narrative at moments of profound theological importance—especially at the cross and the empty tomb.

Feminist, Womanist, and Queer Interpretations

Feminist biblical scholars have long emphasized the need to recover and amplify women's voices in Scripture. Figures such as Elisabeth Schüssler Fiorenza, Amy-Jill Levine, and Sharon Ringe critique the patriarchal assumptions that have shaped both the biblical texts and their interpretation, while also uncovering counter-voices within the Gospels—women who resist, speak, act, and lead. They point out the rhetorical and theological significance of women like the hemorrhaging woman, the woman who anoints Jesus, and the women at the tomb.

Feminist readings also expose the limitations of traditional exegesis, which has too often spiritualized, ignored, or domesticated women's roles. For example, the unnamed woman who anoints Jesus in Mark 14 is described by Jesus as having "done a beautiful thing" and preparing his body for burial. Yet in many readings, her act is dismissed as sentimental or excessive. Feminist interpretation insists on recognizing her as a prophetic witness, one who understands Jesus' death more clearly than his male disciples.

Womanist interpretation, rooted in the experiences of Black women, brings additional dimensions of insight. Scholars such as Renita Weems, Delores Williams, and Wil Gafney explore how race, class, and survival inform the ways in which women are represented in and read the Gospels. Womanist readings pay particular attention to agency in the face of oppression, the power of memory, and the spiritual wisdom of the overlooked. They challenge us to see women not just as passive recipients of grace, but as co-creators of theological insight and active participants in the unfolding of God's story.

Queer readings of the Synoptic Gospels invite further reflection on how assumptions about gender and sexuality shape both the text and its interpretation. Scholars such as Tat-siong Benny Liew and Ken Stone interrogate the ways in which norms of masculinity, family, and social respectability are subverted or reimagined in Jesus' ministry. Jesus' celibacy, his formation of alternative kinship networks, and his embrace of the socially deviant challenge rigid binaries and open space for fluidity, welcome, and redefinition.

These interpretive approaches do not always agree, and they should not be treated as interchangeable. But taken together, they offer a robust, justice-oriented, and theologically fruitful framework for reading the Synoptic Gospels with new attentiveness to the roles of women, the function of gender, and the call to inclusion and liberation in every generation.

Conclusion: Reimagining Discipleship in the Company of Women

The Synoptic Gospels, when read carefully and with awareness of social structures, reveal a world in which power and gender are contested, reconfigured, and reimagined. Jesus does not simply include women in his ministry — he centers them in some of its most pivotal moments. They model faith when others falter, proclaim good news when others are silent, and embody discipleship with courage, insight, and love.

Yet the Gospels also reflect the patriarchal cultures in which they were written. Women are often unnamed, their voices are mediated through others, and their actions are not always given full interpretive weight. The challenge for modern readers is to read these texts with both critical honesty and theological imagination — recognizing both the limits and the liberating potential within the Gospel witness.

To attend to women, gender, and power in the Synoptic Gospels is not to impose modern concerns onto ancient texts. It is to hear more fully the radical edge of Jesus' message, the subversive nature of the kingdom he proclaimed, and the dignity he bestowed on all who followed him — regardless of gender, status, or social expectation.

This work of interpretation matters for the church today. It shapes how we understand leadership, community, embodiment, and voice. It challenges systems that marginalize and silences that exclude. And it calls us to build a community of discipleship that reflects the inclusive, boundary-breaking, justice-loving vision of the one who said, "Whoever does the will of God is my brother and sister and mother" (Mark 3:35).

Chapter 11
Empire, Politics, and Resistance in the Synoptics

Introduction: Gospel in the Shadow of Empire

To read the Synoptic Gospels without attending to their political context is to miss one of their most urgent dimensions. Jesus was not crucified for theological abstraction or mystical insight. He was executed by a Roman governor as a public dissenter — one who disrupted order, drew crowds, and was accused of claiming kingship in a world where only Caesar was king.

The Gospels do not dwell at length on the machinery of Roman rule, but their every page is shaped by its presence. Jesus' ministry takes place under imperial occupation, within a land governed by client kings, tax collectors, and Roman soldiers. Political symbols and tensions — coins bearing Caesar's image, military patrols, elite religious collaboration — permeate the landscape. Against this backdrop, the announcement that "the kingdom of God is at hand" (Mark 1:15) was not simply a spiritual slogan. It was a political claim, one that challenged the narratives, structures, and values of empire.

This chapter explores how the Synoptic Gospels engage with empire — both explicitly and implicitly. It considers how Jesus' teachings, actions, and death interact with Roman power, how the Gospel writers frame his mission in contrast to imperial ideology, and how these texts function as acts of resistance and hope for communities living under oppression. Along the way, we will engage with postcolonial scholarship and theological voices that read the Gospels not as tales of escape, but as narratives of confrontation, courage, and counter-imperial imagination.

The Roman Imperial Context

As discussed in Chapter 3, Roman imperial rule in first-century Palestine was marked by a combination of military power, economic exploitation, and symbolic propaganda. The emperor—whether Augustus, Tiberius, or Nero—was hailed as "Lord," "Savior," "Son of God," and the one who brought peace through victory (*PAX ROMANA*). These titles were not only civic; they were theological, embedded in coinage, temples, inscriptions, and rituals. The Roman system promised security and order—but at the cost of submission, taxation, and elite collaboration.

In Judea and Galilee, Roman rule was enforced through client kings (like Herod the Great and his sons), local magistrates, and ultimately Roman governors like Pontius Pilate. The temple elite—including chief priests and Sadducees—often acted as intermediaries, preserving their own status by maintaining order under Roman oversight. Resistance movements periodically emerged, from the Zealots to apocalyptic prophets, many of whom were swiftly crushed.

It is in this setting that Jesus appears, announcing a different kind of kingdom, performing acts of healing and exorcism, gathering followers, and ultimately being tried and executed under the charge of sedition: "The King of the Jews."

Jesus' Message as Political Challenge

Jesus' central proclamation—"The kingdom of God is at hand"—was both theological and political. The word "kingdom" (*basileia*) resonated with images of authority, rule, and sovereignty. In a world where

Caesar claimed universal dominion, Jesus' message that God's reign was breaking in through him was a radical counter-claim.

His actions reinforced this message. He ate with tax collectors and sinners, undermining systems of purity and exclusion. He healed on the Sabbath, challenging legalistic interpretations and asserting divine authority over sacred time. He drove out demons, not just as exorcisms but as acts of symbolic liberation from oppressive powers. In parables, he described landowners, kings, and stewards—but often inverted expectations, exposing the cruelty and absurdity of systems of domination.

One of the clearest political moments comes in the Temple incident (Mark 11:15–19 and parallels), when Jesus overturns tables and drives out merchants. While often spiritualized as a protest against greed, this act should be seen as a prophetic disruption of an economic and religious system entwined with imperial interests. The temple was not only a sacred site; it was a financial and political hub, collaborating with Rome to collect taxes and maintain control. Jesus' actions here echo Jeremiah's condemnation of the temple as a "den of robbers," and they set the stage for his arrest and execution.

Even Jesus' entry into Jerusalem on a donkey (Mark 11:1–11) is a politically charged parody. In contrast to Roman triumphal processions—complete with horses, armies, and fanfare—Jesus enacts Zechariah's prophecy of a humble king (Zech 9:9), signaling a different kind of power. The crowd's cry, "Hosanna," drawn from Psalm 118, was a plea for salvation and deliverance—a loaded cry under occupation.

The Crucifixion and the Powers

The crucifixion of Jesus is the most explicitly political moment in the Synoptic Gospels. Crucifixion was a Roman method of public execution reserved for political rebels, slaves, and enemies of the state. It was meant not just to kill, but to shame and deter. The charge nailed to the cross — "King of the Jews" — was both mockery and warning.

The passion narratives show how imperial and religious powers collude to silence dissent. Jesus is betrayed, falsely accused, subjected to mockery, torture, and death. Yet even here, the Gospels narrate not the triumph of empire, but its exposure and undoing. The centurion's declaration — "Truly this man was God's Son!" (Mark 15:39) — subverts Roman ideology. The temple veil is torn, the earth quakes, and Jesus, though crucified, is revealed as the true bearer of divine authority.

In Luke's Gospel, Jesus is portrayed as innocent, repeatedly declared guiltless by Pilate and others (Luke 23). He is compared to other executed innocents, like the Maccabean martyrs. Yet Luke also shows Jesus as resolute and prophetic, embracing suffering as the necessary path to redemption and resurrection. The crucifixion becomes not defeat, but the climactic confrontation between God's reign and the forces of death.

Early Christian Resistance and the Gospel's Political Legacy

The political implications of the Synoptic Gospels did not end with Jesus' death. The earliest Christian communities, including those addressed by the Evangelists, lived under ongoing imperial pressure. The language they used — "gospel" (*euangelion*), "Lord," "Savior," "Son of God" — was deeply politicized, echoing and subverting titles claimed by Caesar. To call Jesus "Lord" (Greek: *kurios*) was not only a confession of faith but an act of resistance, a refusal to give ultimate allegiance to the emperor.

These communities gathered in homes, shared meals, cared for the poor, and welcomed strangers — not merely as acts of charity, but as expressions of a countercultural politics rooted in the kingdom of God. The Gospels themselves were shaped in these settings: written for people who knew what it meant to live under surveillance, to experience poverty, to face persecution, and to hope for deliverance.

Throughout the Synoptics, resistance is not always loud or overt — it is often symbolic, embodied, and relational. Jesus teaches his followers to turn the other cheek, walk the extra mile, and love their enemies — not as acquiescence, but as a form of nonviolent disruption. His parables upend social hierarchies. His table fellowship redefines purity. His cross, the empire's tool of terror, becomes the emblem of God's triumph through suffering love.

The political witness of the Synoptic Gospels inspired the early church to practice a form of subversive fidelity: honoring governing authorities where possible (Matt 22:21), but refusing to bow to unjust power. For many, this faithfulness led to martyrdom — not as death for death's sake, but as witness (*martyria*) to a higher allegiance.

Reading the Gospels Politically Today

In modern contexts, the political resonance of the Synoptic Gospels remains as vital as ever. Around the world, Christians read these texts under conditions of oppression, inequality, surveillance, and struggle. In Latin America, Africa, Asia, and marginalized communities in the West, the Gospels are heard not simply as religious texts but as stories of liberation, justice, and alternative power.

Liberation theologians like Gustavo Gutiérrez, Jon Sobrino, and James Cone have insisted that the Gospel demands concrete engagement with structures of oppression. Jesus' identification with the poor, his confrontation with elites, and his execution by empire are not incidental—they are essential to understanding who he is and what discipleship requires.

Contemporary readers are invited to ask: Where does empire still rule today? In what forms do violence, coercion, and domination persist? Who today is crucified by the systems we uphold? And what does it mean to follow a crucified Messiah whose kingdom is not of this world—but is breaking into it through acts of mercy, justice, and truth?

This is not to reduce the Gospel to political ideology. Rather, it is to remember that the kingdom of God is a whole-life vision—a social, economic, spiritual, and embodied transformation. It is a challenge to every empire, ancient or modern, that claims absolute power or trades in fear and exclusion.

Conclusion: The Politics of the Crucified King

The Synoptic Gospels proclaim a kingdom not defined by thrones, armies, or coins, but by compassion, justice, and costly love. They center on a man who renounced coercion, challenged the powerful, embraced the marginalized, and died at the hands of the state. And yet, they declare, this man is Lord—not Caesar.

To read the Gospels faithfully is to enter a story of resistance and renewal, one that invites us to name the powers, stand with the crucified, and live in light of a different reign. It is to hear again Jesus' inaugural words—"The kingdom of God has come near; repent and believe the good news"—not as a call to private piety alone, but as a summons to public allegiance, communal transformation, and courageous discipleship.

In every age, followers of Jesus must ask: Which kingdom do we serve? Whose values shape our lives? What crosses do we ignore, and what tombs do we hope in? The Synoptic Gospels offer no easy answers, but they do offer a path — a narrow way that leads through death to life, through resistance to resurrection, through the empire's shadow to the light of God's peaceable kingdom.

Chapter 12
The Synoptics and Contemporary Culture

Introduction: Ancient Words, Living Witness

The Synoptic Gospels — Matthew, Mark, and Luke — are rooted in a particular time, place, and people. Yet these narratives, composed in the first century in the eastern Mediterranean world, continue to shape the spiritual, ethical, and imaginative lives of communities across the globe. They are more than historical records. They are living texts, animated by the risen Christ and reinterpreted by generations of readers, communities, and cultures.

In this chapter, we explore how the Synoptic Gospels continue to function in contemporary contexts, asking: What role do they play in Christian faith today? How are they engaged — faithfully or distortedly — in modern media and popular culture? What do they say to a world wrestling with injustice, violence, and disorientation? How can they form the moral imagination of communities seeking truth, hope, and transformation?

This chapter is not the conclusion of Gospel study — it is its continuation. For the Synoptic Gospels do not belong only to the past. They speak to the present and call us into the future: into a new way of living, seeing, and being in the world.

The Synoptic Gospels in Christian Faith and Practice

For millions of Christians around the world, the Synoptic Gospels are the spiritual heartbeat of their faith. In liturgies and lectionaries, catechisms and devotional reading, sermons and sacraments, these narratives shape the way believers encounter Jesus and understand the call to discipleship.

Each Gospel contributes distinctively to this formative power. Matthew's Gospel, with its long teaching discourses, including the Sermon on the Mount, provides a sustained ethic for Christian living. Jesus is presented as the authoritative teacher who reinterprets the Torah from the mountaintop, echoing Moses and offering a vision of righteousness rooted in mercy and justice.

Mark's Gospel, in contrast, is often experienced as visceral, urgent, and deeply human. In congregations that wrestle with suffering, doubt, or marginalization, Mark offers a portrayal of Jesus as misunderstood, abandoned, and crucified — but also vindicated in power. Its emphasis on the cost of discipleship and the ambiguity of faith ("I believe; help my unbelief," Mark 9:24) speaks profoundly to those in crisis.

Luke's Gospel, meanwhile, has inspired countless Christians through its attention to the poor, its praise of women, and its sweeping vision of salvation history. Luke's Jesus is prayerful, compassionate, led by the Spirit, and deeply attentive to the excluded. For many global Christian communities, especially those shaped by movements for justice, Luke's message is the most resonant and energizing of the three.

In church life, the Gospels are not only read but performed — in rituals of baptism, Eucharist, and healing; in reenactments of the nativity and passion; and in musical, artistic, and homiletical expression. They provide language for lament and praise, for confession and hope. In individual devotion, believers return again and again to stories like the parable of the sower, the calming of the storm, the call to take up the cross — texts that continue to speak across centuries and continents.

Yet this vitality also requires ongoing interpretation. No reading is neutral. Every encounter with the Gospels is shaped by historical context, theological tradition, and cultural worldview. For the Gospels to remain at the heart of Christian life, they must be read with attentiveness and courage — allowing them not only to comfort but to disturb, not only to affirm but to transform.

The Gospels in Popular Culture and Media

Beyond the walls of churches, the Synoptic Gospels have permeated global culture — appearing in films, literature, music, theater, political rhetoric, protest movements, and even advertising. Their influence on the cultural imagination is massive, though not always faithful to their complexity or intent.

In cinema, Gospel narratives have inspired works ranging from reverent adaptations (*Jesus of Nazareth* & *The Gospel of Matthew*) to provocative reinterpretations (*The Last Temptation of Christ* & *Jesus Christ Superstar*). Each film makes interpretive decisions: which Gospel to follow, how to portray Jesus' character, what emphasis to place on miracles, suffering, resurrection, or teaching. These portrayals shape public perception, especially among those who may never read the Gospels directly.

Recent projects like *The Chosen* aim to humanize the disciples and contextualize Jesus' ministry, often blending Gospel material with imaginative backstory. While this can draw viewers into deeper engagement, it also raises questions about what happens when Scripture is dramatized, serialized, and commercialized. What meanings are emphasized? What is added or omitted? Who controls the portrayal?

In literature, the Gospels have served as source material for spiritual and philosophical reflection.

Writers such as Leo Tolstoy, Toni Morrison, and Marilynne Robinson have engaged Gospel themes to explore forgiveness, grace, suffering, and transformation. In music, references to Gospel narratives appear in works ranging from Handel's *Messiah* to Bob Dylan's gospel period and Kendrick Lamar's prophetic lyrics.

Even in political discourse and advertising, Gospel language is often co-opted. Phrases like "Good Samaritan," "turn the other cheek," or "blessed are the peacemakers" appear in secular settings, often stripped of their theological roots or reinterpreted for ideological ends. This popularization can be powerful — but also problematic, reducing rich texts to slogans.

Thus, engaging the Gospels in culture requires theological literacy and critical engagement. We must ask: What version of Jesus is being portrayed? What vision of the kingdom is being offered? Are the texts being used to liberate or to domesticate, to awaken or to numb?

The Gospels and Contemporary Ethics and Justice

The Synoptic Gospels are not merely concerned with private faith or inner spirituality; they are profoundly moral and political texts, deeply engaged with the structures of society and the patterns of human behavior. Across their pages, we find teachings and actions that speak directly to today's ethical and social challenges — offering not simple answers, but transformative questions and values.

One of the clearest ethical threads in the Gospels is Jesus' persistent concern for economic justice. Again and again, he warns against the dangers of wealth and challenges systems that enrich a few while excluding the many. In the parable of the rich fool (Luke 12:13–21), Jesus exposes the futility of hoarding possessions in the face of mortality and divine judgment. In Matthew's Sermon on the Mount (Matt 6:19–24), he urges his followers to store up treasure in heaven, warning that where one's treasure is, there the heart will be also. His interactions with the rich man in Mark 10 and with Zacchaeus in Luke 19 show that discipleship demands not only inner conversion but concrete economic change — releasing wealth, redistributing resources, and responding generously to the needs of others.

Alongside this, the Gospels offer a sharp critique of systemic injustice and hypocrisy, particularly among those in positions of religious or social power. Jesus denounces leaders who use their status to burden others while avoiding the demands of mercy and compassion. In Matthew 23, he delivers a searing indictment of scribes and Pharisees who perform piety for public acclaim while neglecting what he calls "the weightier matters of the law: justice and mercy and faith." These confrontations are not simply personal — they are structural, aimed at a system that elevates ritual over relationship, control over care.

Equally prominent is Jesus' practice of radical inclusion and hospitality. In all three Synoptic Gospels, Jesus consistently welcomes those who are excluded, whether because of gender, ethnicity, illness, occupation, or moral judgment. He dines with tax collectors and sinners, speaks with women in public, touches lepers, heals Gentiles, and makes Samaritans and widows heroes in his parables. In Luke's Gospel especially, this openness is part of a larger vision of reversal, where the lowly are lifted up and the proud are brought down. In today's world — rife with xenophobia, racism, misogyny, and fear of the "other" — the Gospels call the church to become a community of embrace, not exclusion.

The Gospels also offer a profound critique of violence and domination. Jesus teaches non-retaliation in the face of injury ("turn the other cheek"), urges love for enemies, and refuses to use force even when threatened with arrest and death. His triumph is not military but sacrificial; his enthronement comes through the cross. In a culture saturated with violence—from militarism and gun culture to carceral systems and abusive authority—the Gospels invite Christians to imagine a different kind of power: one rooted in vulnerability, nonviolence, and redemptive suffering.

These ethical dimensions are not abstract ideals; they are meant to be lived. The Gospels have been a wellspring of inspiration for movements of justice and liberation throughout history. From abolitionists quoting the Exodus and the Beatitudes, to civil rights leaders like Martin Luther King Jr. preaching the Sermon on the Mount, to modern advocates for immigration reform, prison abolition, economic equity, and climate justice, the Gospels have animated vision and action.

Yet they have also been misused—deployed to justify hierarchy, patriarchy, colonialism, and oppression. As such, reading the Synoptic Gospels today requires discernment, contextual awareness, and ethical responsibility. They are not ethical manuals in the modern sense, nor do they offer ready-made policy prescriptions. Rather, they provide a vision of the world as it is meant to be—a world where mercy outruns judgment, where strangers are welcomed, where wealth is shared, and where peace is pursued at any cost.

To read the Synoptic Gospels in our time is to hear not only a word of comfort, but a call to action, solidarity, and transformation. Their moral power lies not in legalism, but in the vision they offer: the inbreaking of God's reign in the midst of human injustice—a kingdom where the first are last, and the last are finally seen, heard, and honored.

Conclusion: A Living Word for a Changing World

The Synoptic Gospels are not finished. Though the ink on the manuscripts is dry, the story they tell is still unfolding. In every act of reading, teaching, protesting, forgiving, healing, and hoping, the Gospel is lived again. Its truth is not confined to the past but breaks open in the present—wherever people hunger for justice, healing, belonging, and grace.

In a world of rapid change, rising fear, and profound injustice, these ancient texts offer courage and clarity. They center the poor and marginalized, challenge the powerful, and announce a kingdom not of dominance but of peace. They proclaim a God who walks among the wounded, who eats with sinners, and who defeats death not with violence but with love.

To read the Synoptic Gospels today is to encounter a radical invitation—to turn from despair and domination, and to follow the way of Jesus: crucified, risen, and alive among us. It is to enter a story that is still being written—by artists and activists, pastors and prisoners, teachers and children, saints and sinners alike.

May we, too, find our place in that story. And may the words of the Gospels—ancient, sharp, beautiful, and true—become in us a living word.